The

EVERYTHING®
Wills & Estate Planning Book

Dear Reader:

Writing a will and planning an estate can be a daunting undertaking and requires the most accurate and up-to-date information possible. I am confident that my formal education, teaching experience, and tried and tested advice is well suited for the task.

I graduated first in my class from the Thomas M. Cooley Law School in 1978. After five years of private practice, I was asked to join the faculty at Cooley Law School as a full-time law professor. During my seventeen-year tenure, I taught wills, trusts, income tax, and estate planning to thousands of law students. As any professor will tell you, there is no greater education than the one you receive teaching others.

I left the law school and returned to the full-time practice of law and immediately discovered that clients appreciated my educational style and practical experience. They tell me about their families, I teach them the rules, and they participate in crafting a plan that meets their needs. I've learned something new from each of my clients, and I'm happy to pass my years of knowledge and experience on to you. Read closely, plan carefully, and get on with the excitement and wonder of living.

Sincerely,

Kimberly A. Colgate

The EVERYTHING® Series

Editorial

Publishing Director	Gary M. Krebs
Managing Editor	Kate McBride
Copy Chief	Laura MacLaughlin
Acquisitions Editor	Eric Hall
Development Editor	Lesley Bolton
Production Editor	Khrysti Nazzaro

Production

Production Director	Susan Beale
Production Manager	Michelle Roy Kelly
Series Designers	Daria Perreault
	Colleen Cunningham
Cover Design	Paul Beatrice
	Frank Rivera
Layout and Graphics	Colleen Cunningham
	Rachael Eiben
	Michelle Roy Kelly
	Daria Perreault
	Erin Ring
Series Cover Artist	Barry Littmann

THE
EVERYTHING®
WILLS &
ESTATE PLANNING
BOOK

Professional advice to safeguard your
assets and provide security for your family

Kimberly A. Colgate

Adams Media Corporation
Avon, Massachusetts

To my children: Rodney and Cheryl Miles.

An Everything® Series Book.
Everything® is a registered trademark of Adams Media Corporation.

Published by Adams Media Corporation
57 Littlefield Street, Avon, MA 02322 U.S.A.
www.adamsmedia.com

ISBN: 1-58062-880-X
Printed in the United States of America.

J I H G F E D C B A

Library of Congress Cataloging-in-Publication Data
Colgate, Kimberly A.
The everything wills & estate planning book / Kimberly A. Colgate.
p.   cm.   (An everything series book)
ISBN 1-58062-880-X
1. Wills–United States. 2. Estate planning–United States.
I. Title: Everything wills and estate planning book. II. Title. III.
Series: Everything series.
KF755.C65   2003
346.7305'2—dc21   2003000373

This publication is designed to provide accurate and authoritative information with regard to
the subject matter covered. It is sold with the understanding that the publisher is not engaged
in rendering legal, accounting, or other professional advice. If legal advice or other expert
assistance is required, the services of a competent professional person should be sought.
—From a *Declaration of Principles* jointly adopted by a Committee of the American Bar
Association and a Committee of Publishers and Associations

Many of the designations used by manufacturers and sellers to distinguish their products are
claimed as trademarks. Where those designations appear in this book and Adams Media was
aware of a trademark claim, the designations have been printed with initial capital letters.

The Everything® Wills & Estate Planning Book does not purport to render legal advice as
many laws are particular to individual states. Readers should consult a legal professional for
such advice.

This book is available at quantity discounts for bulk purchases.
For information, call 1-800-872-5627.

Contents

cknowledgments

I would like to acknowledge the
Thomas M. Cooley Law School;
its commitment to practical legal scholarship
gave me the skills to write this book

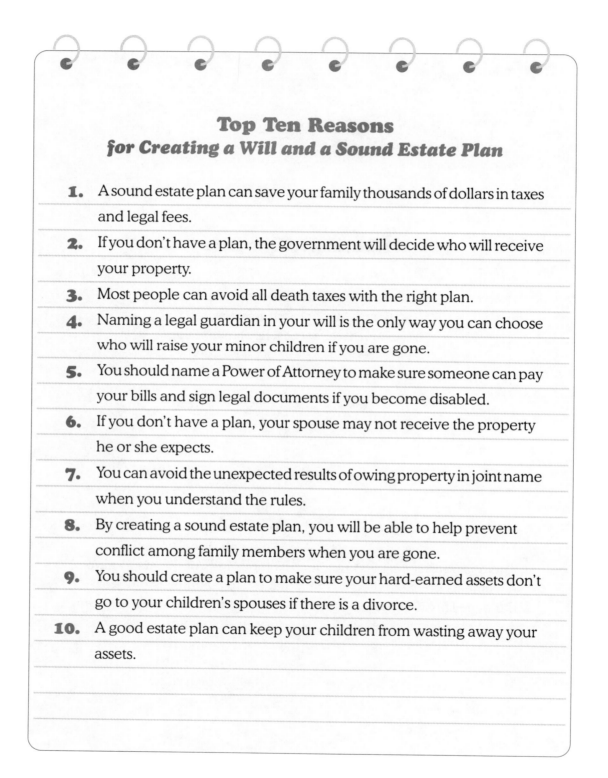

Top Ten Reasons
for Creating a Will and a Sound Estate Plan

1. A sound estate plan can save your family thousands of dollars in taxes and legal fees.

2. If you don't have a plan, the government will decide who will receive your property.

3. Most people can avoid all death taxes with the right plan.

4. Naming a legal guardian in your will is the only way you can choose who will raise your minor children if you are gone.

5. You should name a Power of Attorney to make sure someone can pay your bills and sign legal documents if you become disabled.

6. If you don't have a plan, your spouse may not receive the property he or she expects.

7. You can avoid the unexpected results of owing property in joint name when you understand the rules.

8. By creating a sound estate plan, you will be able to help prevent conflict among family members when you are gone.

9. You should create a plan to make sure your hard-earned assets don't go to your children's spouses if there is a divorce.

10. A good estate plan can keep your children from wasting away your assets.

Introduction

▶ WHAT ARE THE MOST IMPORTANT THINGS IN LIFE? Most responses include family, health, love, home, and financial security. Everyone works very hard to achieve his or her dreams and goals. And yet, most people avoid one of the most important steps for the future—planning for the security of their family after they are gone.

There are three reasons why most people don't plan. First, for hundreds of years the average person has been led to believe that families should not discuss wills, trusts, and the probate process. Some people believe that there is a secret process that must happen when someone passes away. In fact, when you learn the rules and prepare, you will find that there is no secret to the process. You will discover that your property can pass to your loved ones seamlessly. *The Everything® Wills & Estate Planning Book* takes the mystery out of the planning process and teaches you how to prepare for your family's security and peace of mind.

The second reason most people don't plan is because they don't want to spend the money to have a will or a trust prepared. There is a misconception that it costs thousands of dollars to have documents prepared. People think that estate planning is only for the rich. This is simply not true. When you know the rules, you can create documents yourself or have a lawyer help you in a very cost-efficient manner. The fact of the matter is, it is not expensive to create an estate plan—what is expensive is to die without a plan. You will learn the rules about how to create a plan that will save you thousands, perhaps hundreds of thousands, of dollars.

The third reason most people don't plan is because they are intimidated or afraid. The words are unfamiliar, making delicate decisions even more difficult to make. This book will teach you the rules and the meanings of those confusing words, allowing you to create a plan that makes sense for your family.

The Everything® Wills & Estate Planning Book carefully guides you through the decisions you need to make before you have documents prepared. It teaches you about the different types of documents that are available and gives you suggestions as to which documents might best meet the needs of your family. While you are planning for the future, you will discover that the planning process may even help you save money that your family can enjoy now.

Unfortunately, most families learn a painful lesson when someone they know or love passes away without a plan. The death of a loved one is the event that motivates most people to prepare their own estate-planning documents. By following the suggestions provided, you will avoid that crisis for your family.

This book guides you step by step through the planning process. It teaches you the rules on each topic and empowers you to make the necessary decisions for your family in a cost-efficient manner. But more importantly, it teaches you that planning for tomorrow can help create a better today. Ⓔ

Chapter 1

Why You Should Plan

There are many reasons, both emotional and financial, for having a sound estate plan. It really doesn't matter how old you are; your family and loved ones will suffer when you leave them. While that cannot be helped, if you prepare, you can spare them a great deal of additional grief and expense.

Planning Is for Everyone

Your family and loved ones will suffer an enormous amount of grief when they lose you. If you don't have a plan and are not prepared, your family has to dig through your belongings to find the information they need after you are gone—further reminding them of their loss. There are many things that need to be done that you don't think about until you have experienced the loss of a loved one.

Planning in Your Twenties

You may think you don't need to plan because, after all, you're only twenty years old. The chance that something will happen to you is very slim, but if it does, your family will have a lot to do. Everyone at any age should have certain legal documents in place. The most important of these are a medical designate and a living will.

If you should become injured, a medical designate is the person who will make medical decisions on your behalf. A living will is a legal document that expresses your wishes regarding whether or not you want your life artificially prolonged in the event that you are permanently incapacitated with no chance of recovery. This may seem morbid, but if you have strong feelings about life support you should be prepared.

You should also consider preparing a will at this age. You may not have a lot of belongings, but it will be much easier for your family if you have a document stating how you want your property to be distributed.

The amount of planning you need to do for your property will depend on how much property you have. Chapter 2 includes steps to take to help you determine whether you need something more than a will.

Congratulations! You Just Had a Baby

One of the most important decisions you will ever make (besides whether or not to have a baby) is who will take care of your baby if you are gone. If something happens to you, your spouse will become the legal guardian of your child. If something happens to both of you, someone will have to be given the responsibility of raising your child. Wouldn't you like to be the one to decide just who that someone will be?

The only document that allows you to name a guardian for your baby, if both you and your spouse are gone, is your will. Most young parents don't—or don't want to—think about this possibility. However, it is a very important matter concerning the well-being of your child, so it's best to be prepared—just in case.

The Children Have Left the Nest

When the children are all gone to college or have moved out of the house, parents' lives change dramatically. The daily planning associated with teenagers has ended and perhaps been replaced with long-distance telephone bills.

When your children leave home, it is an excellent time to evaluate your goals. You will probably think more about retirement. This is the perfect time to take a serious look at your estate plan. You are at a point in your life when you have likely accumulated a lot of things and have not had time to evaluate what would happen to these things if you were gone. And more importantly, you've probably not had the time until now to assess whether you are making the best use of your property and investments. Creating an estate plan will help you do just that.

Entering Retirement

Retirement is the time when most people take a long look at their estate plan. If you decided to retire, you probably took the time to gather most of the information you needed to evaluate your estate plan. This involves calculating how much money you have and whether you will have enough money coming in to retire from your job. This is an excellent time to complete the planning process. After all, you've already gotten started; why not just finish the job?

The Golden Years

Every single person in his or her golden years has known someone who has died. The stories about the cost, delay, and turmoil are probably the general rule and not the exception. It doesn't have to be like this. Many times people think they are prepared, and unfortunately when it is too late, it is discovered that the plan was not as complete as everyone thought. Put your mind at rest and do what you can now to ensure a well-organized and comprehensive plan.

One of the reasons people don't prepare when they are in their golden years is because they don't want to make an appointment with a professional and talk about death. Another reason people avoid planning is because it is frustrating and expensive to try to figure out what needs to be done. This book will solve both of these concerns.

Protecting Your Family

The most important reason for you to plan, regardless of where you are in the cycle of life, is to protect your family. The issues that face you at different points of your life change. For instance, as you mature, there are usually more family members who depend on you. The modern family is more complicated than it was in the old days when Mom stayed home and raised the children, Dad went to work, and, after the children left home, Mom and Dad started planning for retirement. This picture has changed dramatically.

Your Spouse

When you think about your spouse, you should consider whether there is anyone who might create difficulties for, or take advantage of, him or her when you pass on. For example, when you are newly married, if something happens to you, it is not uncommon for your relatives to be resentful about what your new bride or groom owns and where the property came from. These disagreements can be about small items that relatives feel belong to them or over major financial issues. You need to protect your spouse by at least having a will that defines the property that belongs to your spouse and that which belongs to your relatives.

If you have been married for a long period of time, it could be your own children who disagree with your spouse's wishes. When this happens, it is usually because your spouse has a soft spot in his or her heart for one or more of your children. When you have more than one child, your children have different needs. Just as you may have argued about what your children should or should not have when you were there, these emotional pulls often heighten after you are gone.

You may want to put a plan in place that will help your spouse say no to your relatives and your own children. The more complex your property holdings, the more important it is for you to plan ahead for these contingencies.

Remarriage

If this is a second marriage for you, there are bombshells you might not have expected. There may be children from your former marriage or children from your spouse's former marriage who can complicate matters. Conflicting interests may emerge after you are gone. Perhaps you avoid putting a plan in place because it is difficult for you to address these competing needs. But just imagine how difficult it will be for your spouse to make important decisions after you are gone.

ALERT!

Oftentimes, people create a plan that leaves all of their property to their spouses, believing that the surviving spouse will take care of the children. Though this may sound reasonable, it may not be the best plan. Your children may put pressure on your spouse and cause tension among family members. Or the spouse may not act as you thought he or she would.

It is better if you and your spouse can develop a plan together, but if you need to seek counsel and put a plan in place without discussing your plan with your family, at least everyone will know what you wanted after you are gone. When you are involved in a second marriage, it is imperative that you put a plan in place to protect everyone involved—your spouse and your other family members and loved ones.

Your Children

If both you and your spouse pass on and do not leave a plan, your property will be distributable to your children, but not necessarily distributed in the way that you would wish. This could also create tension among siblings.

When you think about what would happen to your property if both you and your spouse are gone, or if you are not married and have children, you should think about when your children should receive your property after your death. You should consider the age of your children, their maturity, and whether inheriting all or a share of your property would promote responsibility in them.

If your children are minors, without a different plan in place, the person who becomes the legal guardian of your children will have control of their money and property. You should think about whether that guardian will make the best financial choices on behalf of your children.

If your children are in their twenties or thirties, you should consider whether they will pursue their education if they receive an inheritance (if that is important to you) and whether they will make the best choices. You are going to learn that there are ways you can help protect your children, but it takes some thought and planning.

FACT

If your child receives an inheritance from you, you might wonder what happens to the inheritance if there is a divorce. The divorce laws in most states provide that inherited property is not marital property. But there are a lot of exceptions to this rule. Establishing trusts for your children will protect the inherited property.

Your Grandchildren

When you evaluate your property and the needs of your children and your grandchildren, you may want to create a plan that leaves some money or property for the benefit of your grandchildren. Sometimes when you leave a small inheritance for a grandchild, it can have a dramatic impact on her or his future. For instance, you can encourage your grandchild to attend college by setting up a fund that can be spent only for educational purposes. Many states have started prepaid college funds. Some state funds require that the child attend a college located in the state where the fund was created. Other states allow the fund to be used in some manner, typically at a discount, in another state. Most funds even allow you to name someone who can use the benefit if the child does not use the funds to attend college. If such funds interest you, check on the availability of a college fund in your state and the limitations that fund may have.

If you want to provide maximum flexibility, you can establish a trust for your grandchildren from which funds are disbursed only for educational purposes. For instance, if your grandchild does not attend college, the funds can then be spent on another grandchild who does want to attend college.

FACT

If you left your grandchild $10,000 and the money was invested for fifteen years at 10 percent, your grandchild would have roughly $43,997 to use toward college or some other worthy investment.

Protecting Your Assets from Creditors

Protecting yourself from creditors while you are alive is quite different from protecting your family from creditors after you are gone. In most states, if you own or control property, your creditors can access your property to pay outstanding bills. Of course, there are exceptions to this rule in every state. Some states protect your home from creditors while others protect certain types of investments. Almost all states protect your retirement plan.

As you will learn in later chapters, after you are gone, it is a different game. You can create trusts that will give your family the benefit of the income from your property and even distributions of the property itself, and the trusts will keep creditors from touching that property. (When you finish reading the chapters about trusts, if asset protection is important to you, you should organize the information concerning your assets and make an appointment with an asset protection lawyer, who can answer specific questions regarding your state's laws.)

ALERT!

It can be very difficult for your family and loved ones to keep your hard-earned assets if you do not have a plan. You can substantially reduce the costs and save taxes if you are organized and understand what happens to your assets after you are gone.

Avoiding Probate Costs

Most people don't understand that if you have a will, your family still needs to go through the probate process to distribute the property you owned. Even so, when you have a will, it reduces the cost of probate because the will provides instructions about how your property should be distributed. If you don't have a will, your state law will govern who gets your property.

There are certain things you can do to save taxes and avoid the cost and delay of probate, but you must plan for it. The key is to understand the options, and then you will be in a position to make the right choices for your family. Chapters 4 and 5 will delve deeper into the probate process, but, for now, keep in mind that this is one way in which your careful planning and preparation will come into play.

Reducing Taxes

Believe it or not, to protect your family and loved ones, you will need to concern yourself with the issue of taxes after you pass on. Primarily, you will want to focus on income taxes and death taxes.

The rules about income taxes on property that is received by someone when you die are very tricky. One small mistake can cost your family thousands, perhaps hundreds of thousands, of dollars. The rules about what property is subject to income tax and how you can reduce or eliminate that tax by owning your property in a different way are complicated but rewarding. Don't fret, you will learn these income tax rules and get tips on how you might create a plan to minimize the income tax consequences to your family and in many cases even ✗ eliminate income taxes on inherited property.

Death taxes are a strange creature. The laws about taxes that are owed when you die are complex. But like most topics that are complex, if the presentation is broken down into bite-sized pieces and you are given examples about how each piece works, you can understand death taxes and plan your estate to minimize those taxes or avoid them altogether.

When you understand how you need to prepare—the decisions you need to make and the possible solutions—it reduces the cost of having to get something fixed. Each chapter is designed to teach you rules that would cost $150 to $200, or more, per hour to learn from a lawyer. Even if you need to hire a lawyer to prepare your documents, by being educated you will save an enormous amount of time and money in the long run.

Those who hire lawyers to draft documents often eliminate or lessen the federal death taxes; however, they have paid substantial lawyer's fees in the process. When you are organized and understand the tax rules yourself, you can enjoy the same benefits while paying less in lawyer costs.

Making Your Dreams Live On

A well-designed plan can make your dreams live on. If you don't have a plan, your family might not know what your dream was. Or even if the dream was known, it may not be realized due to a big chunk of your money and property being spent on legal fees and taxes that could have been saved if you had understood the rules and had a plan in place.

Wills, trusts, probate, annuities, and retirement plans are all tools used to make your dreams live on. You will soon learn what tools you have to work with and how to use them to their maximum effect. While some of these tools are designed to help after you are gone, some of them will help you accumulate more while you are living. Learn the rules, and let your dreams live on! (E)

Chapter 2

Preplan Prerequisites

Becoming familiar with the rules and what strategies are available to you during the preplanning stages will save you and your loved ones a substantial sum of money. More importantly, you will be able to rest assured that you have found a plan that both carries out your wishes and protects your loved ones after you have passed on.

Know What Is Available

Before you can create a plan that will provide for your family and loved ones, you need to know what types of documents and legal arrangements are available to you. Some documents are easier to create now, but are more expensive for your family and loved ones after you are gone. Other documents are more challenging to create now, but will save your family and loved ones a substantial amount of money.

There are four ways you can pass property to your loved ones: a will, a trust, joint property, and certain types of contracts. Each of these documents or legal arrangements has advantages and disadvantages.

Get to Know the Will

A will is the easiest and cheapest estate-planning document to prepare. Most people can create their own will without hiring a lawyer. After you are gone, your will must be probated. Probate is a process whereby your loved ones must petition the local probate court, open a probate file, administer the property pursuant to your state's probate code, and then distribute the property. If you haven't already guessed, it is almost impossible for a family to probate a will without hiring a lawyer. Probate is like a lawsuit. There are detailed court rules and forms required to effectively probate a will.

The main disadvantage to using a will is that there are additional costs and delays associated with the process after you are gone. However, if you have a will, at least you have left instructions about how you want your property distributed.

The Document for Young Families

A will may be the document of choice for a young family for several reasons. The first reason is that a will is the only document that allows you to name a guardian for your minor children. It is not necessary to name a guardian if there is a natural parent living. However, if both natural parents are gone, a will gives you the opportunity to choose the person or persons you would like to raise your children. If you do not have a will, and both natural parents are gone, the probate court will conduct hearings to determine who should serve as the legal guardian of your minor children. A person who petitions the court to serve as legal guardian may not be the person you would have chosen had you prepared for this eventuality in advance. If this thought scares you, keep in mind that it is very difficult for someone to contest your choice of a guardian when you name that person in your will.

The second reason a young person or family might choose to have a will rather than a different document or legal arrangement is because a will is easy and inexpensive to prepare. A young person is less likely to die than someone older. Even so, in the unlikely event of a premature death, it is important that your instructions are contained in a legally binding document. If you don't have a will, every state has a law that directs how your property will pass when you are gone, and this distribution may not fit with your intentions.

FACT

By becoming familiar with estate planning, you can reduce the need for a lawyer by doing most of the work yourself. The average attorney charges $175 per hour. If you save your lawyer ten hours of time, you have saved $1,750!

Uncomplicated Affairs

If you are older, you may choose to have a will because your affairs are not complex, but you want to make sure that your property passes to the loved ones of your choice. If you are not concerned about the expense of distributing your assets when you are gone, a will is an excellent estate-planning document.

Consider the Advantages of a Trust

Why would you have a trust as opposed to a will? Like a will, your property will be distributed according to the instructions you place in the document. But the added bonus is that your loved ones will not have to use the probate process, saving them a tremendous amount of money and time.

Establish a Management Plan

You may also choose to use a trust because you don't want your property distributed immediately when you are gone. Creating a trust allows you to establish a management plan for your family. Assets in a trust are distributed according to a predetermined schedule.

There are many reasons why you might not want your property distributed right away. You may be concerned that your spouse is not capable of managing the property, or if both you and your spouse are gone, your children will be too young to receive your property. You may not want the legal guardian of your children to have control of your property. Or perhaps you are worried that your children's creditors or spouse will try to lay claim to your property when you are gone. A trust allows you to protect against all of these risks. You will learn how to create a trust and how easy it is to change in a later chapter.

Choose the Trustee

Many people think you have to involve a bank in order to have a trust. This is not true. You can serve as trustee while you are living, then choose a family member or other loved one to serve as trustee after you are gone. A bank needn't be involved, unless, of course, you want one to be.

You can place instructions in the trust document that will guide your trustee on how to manage your property. The instructions can be very flexible, granting a trustee the power to distribute property when the trustee feels it is appropriate, or the trust document can set out very specific instructions that must be followed.

FACT

If your estate is subject to federal death taxes, you will probably want to consider using a trust. A trust will reduce the death taxes owed by your estate. Trusts are extremely flexible legal documents. There are a few more steps involved to create the trust, but there is little or no cost to your family or loved ones after you are gone.

Appreciate the Convenience of Joint Property

Owning your property in joint name with another person is also a simple estate plan. The primary advantage to owning property in joint name is that title passes automatically to the surviving joint tenant when you die. This means your joint tenant doesn't have to hire a lawyer to probate your property after your death.

Many parents put a child's name on property. For example, they may add a child's name to a bank account. This is often done for convenience, to allow that child to assist with bill paying and banking. However, let's say the parent has a will that says, "Divide all of my property equally among my children." The parent thinks the will controls and overrides joint-property rules. That is not true! The joint property, in this case a bank account, belongs only to the child whose name is on the account. You might believe or hope that the child named on the account would divide the property with his or her siblings, but that is not always the case. You need to be careful with joint property.

ALERT!

It is important for you to understand that your will has absolutely no effect on who receives property that is held in joint name with you and someone else. The property automatically passes to the joint tenant. A major disadvantage to owning property in joint name can be increased income taxes and possibly death taxes that could have been avoided.

Beware of Contractual Arrangements

Many people think that all their property will be divided in equal shares among their children if they have a will or a trust that says, "I hereby leave all of my property in equal shares to my children." Unfortunately, this is not always the case. A will or a trust has no effect on how certain types of property are distributed. There are four types of property that pass according to the terms of the contract and are not affected by your will.

- Life insurance
- Annuities
- IRAs and retirement accounts
- Certain business contracts

Life insurance and annuities are paid to the person you named as a beneficiary when you purchased them. Both of these types of property are paid according to the terms of the contract. Sometimes people have the same misunderstanding about life insurance and annuities as they do about joint property. People tend to think that a will or a trust controls all of their property. You will find as you proceed through the process of planning that you need to evaluate how each piece of property, including life insurance and annuities, will be paid when you are gone.

IRAs (Individual Retirement Account) and retirement accounts are also paid to the person you named as a beneficiary. Your will or trust will have no effect on who receives those benefits. Also, more complex business contracts for partnerships and corporations often have buy-out provisions that will control and cause the partnership or corporate stock to be excluded from the probate process.

There is no one right plan. Learning the rules will help you choose the best legal documents and types of property ownership that will meet the goals of your family and loved ones.

Make Your Wish List

Before you can create your plan, you need to know what you're working with. Buy a three-ring binder or notebook, a set of divider tabs, a package of three-hole-punch paper, a pencil, a pencil sharpener, and an eraser. These are the supplies you will need to create your plan. A three-ring binder or notebook is important because you will likely add or remove sheets of paper quite often. Your plan will be divided into categories and organized in a way that will help you make the best decisions.

Who

The first tab of your notebook will be used to define who will be part of your plan. List everyone you want included on one sheet of paper— your spouse, children, grandchildren, parents, and perhaps your community. Then, make a separate sheet of paper for each person or entity to whom you plan to leave property. Write down all of the basic information about each person on the separate pieces of paper, including the person's full legal name, relationship to you, birth date, social security number, address, telephone number, and e-mail address.

Who you include in your plan may change as you continue through the planning process. Or circumstances may change for your loved ones. You may find yourself using that eraser to eliminate a name from the master list or adding a sheet of paper for someone you forgot.

The reason you want to use a separate piece of paper for each person or entity is because you are going to create a miniplan for each, allowing you to make notes or record any special needs. You will also have to decide what happens to that person's share if he or she is gone. Should his share go to his children, your siblings, or another person? Create a flow chart for each person's share.

What

The next tabs in your notebook should be used to summarize and describe your property. Make a separate tab for each category of property you own, such as:

- Real estate
- Stocks
- Bonds
- Mutual funds
- Life insurance
- Retirement accounts and annuities
- Bank accounts

Each piece of property gets its own sheet of paper. List the value of the property, the amount of debt against the property, what you paid for the property, and the cost of any improvements you have made. This core information is important to help you make decisions about the property. You don't need to have your property appraised. A fair estimate of the value of the property is typically sufficient to begin your plan.

Once you have all the information down, you will learn to analyze it in various ways. It will not only help you decide how you are going to distribute your property, but it will also help you make critical decisions about the income tax consequences and the estate and gift tax consequences of your choices.

FACT

Making decisions about your property is like playing a game. Each piece of paper that describes your property can be moved around as if the property were on a game board.

Where, When, and Why

Now you can think about where, when, and why. The decisions you make about one or more pieces of your property may change when you start thinking about the needs of your loved ones, the practical ramifications of what your loved ones would do with your property, and the tax consequences associated with your choices.

For example, assume you own a vacation cottage. You recorded the value of the cottage, what you paid for it, and the cost of any improvements made, and you placed this information in your notebook. Now list the annual operating costs, such as utilities, taxes, and normal upkeep of the cottage on the same piece of paper.

When you start asking yourself who should receive your cottage and why, your initial decision about the cottage might change. Let's say you started the planning process thinking you would divide all of your property equally among your children. But when you focus on the information you have about the cottage, you realize how difficult it would be for your children to own the property together. You should think about who is going to pay the bills, who will maintain the cottage, and whether one child will use the cottage more than another. Your children may fight over whether or not the cottage should be sold. Maybe your children are too young to maintain the cottage. Perhaps one child is better equipped to own the cottage. You are now beginning to analyze not only who and what, but where, when, and why as well.

For fun, keep track of the number of hours you spend getting organized and making basic family decisions. Imagine how much it would cost if you paid a lawyer to gather the information about your family and your assets. Multiply the number of hours by $175 per hour and be pleased about the money you have saved!

When you take all of the sheets of paper representing the property you own and lay them out on the table, it may make more sense to leave your personal residence to one child, your cottage to another, and divide the investments among the remaining children. Your children's needs and what they are capable of managing are often quite different for each child.

The process of organizing your property piece by piece helps to crystallize the decisions you make for your family. As you think through your choices, you may find yourself changing your mind about who should receive that piece of property or when the property should be distributed. Remember, those pieces of paper can come in and out of the three-ring binder. Also, as you learn the rules about what legal arrangements you can use, you may change your mind about who, what, where, when, and why.

Shop for a Lawyer

People price-shop for almost everything they buy. Yet most people don't price-shop for a lawyer. This is because most don't know how—where to look and what to ask. If this describes you, read on.

The best way to find a lawyer is a referral from a satisfied client. Ask your friends, neighbors, and work colleagues if they have had any planning done. Ask who they used, how much it cost, and whether they were satisfied with the results. If you don't find a lawyer this way, contact your local or state bar association. Many of the state bar associations have a referral service or a directory that will help you find a lawyer in your area who does estate planning.

When you find a lawyer, it is important to understand what he or she will do for you. A lawyer does different things for you when helping you plan than what he or she does after you are gone.

Planning

Your lawyer spends the least amount of time drafting documents for you. Most of your lawyer's time is spent learning about your family and your property and informing you of your options. Your lawyer does five things for you:

1. Learns about your property
2. Learns about your family
3. Learns what you want to do with your property
4. Explains the law
5. Drafts documents to implement your plan

If you are organized and have played the who, what, where, when, and why game, you have done most of the lawyer's job. Then, when you learn the rules about the various legal documents you can use, you have done another part of your lawyer's job. Imagine how much money you have saved. You can then make an appointment with your lawyer, and the only job left is to have your lawyer prepare the documents.

Post-Death Tasks

The functions a lawyer will perform for your loved ones after you are gone depend on what type of documents you had in place. If you had a will, the lawyer will start a probate proceeding in your county probate court. If you didn't have a will (or any other estate-planning document), the steps the lawyer needs to take are almost the same. The difference is that your state's laws will determine who takes your property. (The particulars regarding the probate process are covered in Chapter 4.)

If you have used a trust, a lawyer might be necessary to explain to the trustee his or her duties. But frankly, if you are organized and understand your documents, you will be able to explain the duties to your trustee while you are living, preparing your trustee to serve as your successor trustee after you are gone.

FACT

The biggest misconception about wills is that most people think that if you have a will, there will be no probate. This is not true. In order to avoid probate, you need to have documents in place other than a will, such as a trust or jointly owned property.

If your estate is subject to federal death taxes, you will need to hire either a lawyer or an accountant to prepare the federal death tax return. It is impossible for a person to prepare the federal death tax return without professional help. A federal death tax return is over fifty pages long and has terms and phrases that even many lawyers don't understand. You will need to hire a lawyer or an accountant who prepares federal death tax returns on a regular basis. He or she will also need to file the final income tax returns.

ESSENTIAL

The lawyer will typically arrange to close credit cards, terminate social security, secure final wages, and pay final expenses. You can do many of these tasks yourself, with some guidance from the lawyer. This will save you money.

Questions You Should Ask

When you contact the lawyer's office, find out if the initial consultation or meeting is free—this is a common practice. Ask the lawyer how long he or she plans for the first meeting and what information you should bring. If the lawyer tells you that you have a half-hour appointment and you don't need to bring anything to the meeting, you can be sure you won't get much information for free: You are being invited to be sold on the lawyer's services.

Request information about the firm to be sent in advance of your appointment. Having information on the firm readily available is often a sign of a well-organized professional. The information does not have to be glossy and expensive, but it should be informative. Find out if there is a Web site describing the firm. A nicely presented Web site indicates that the lawyer is on top of technology. This can be important because a technologically sophisticated office typically saves you money. Ask the lawyer how many areas of law he or she covers. If the answer is all areas of the law, this is probably not the lawyer you want to draft your plan. It is impossible to be an expert in every area of law.

Let the Interrogation Begin!

Ask the lawyer a few basic planning questions and be prepared with the answers yourself, in order to better evaluate him or her. For instance, you might ask, "What is the main disadvantage to owning property in joint name?" The answer is that when you own property in joint name, **X** there can be negative income tax consequences for the surviving joint tenant. Or you could ask, "If property is placed in a revocable trust, does the trust protect the property from creditors?" The answer is no. As long as you hold a power to revoke the trust, creditors can reach the assets held in trust.

If the lawyer does not know the answers, or tells you that he or she has to get back with you, this is not the lawyer you want. If the lawyer is offended that you are asking questions, then you'll likely want to look elsewhere.

Should You Ask How Much?

Yes. You should definitely ask how much it will cost. The answer to this question is often, "Well, it depends." Don't let it rest at that. Follow up with more specific questions. Find out if the lawyer bills by the hour, by the project, or by the nature of the documents prepared. If the lawyer charges by the hour, find out what the hourly fee is.

It is also important to ask if other people in the office will be working on your file. Different lawyers in a firm typically have different billing rates. Find out whether the bills will list who worked on your file and how much each person billed per hour. You should also ask if a paralegal will be working on your file. If so, how much will you be billed per hour for the paralegal's work? Then ask how many hours the lawyer thinks each person will be spending on your job. Don't feel as though you are being intrusive or demanding. This is your money, and you have a right to know where it goes.

ALERT!

Sometimes law firms include separate charges for filing costs, photocopies, telephone charges, or research time. Be sure to inquire about each of these. It isn't a pleasant surprise to get a bill for several hundred dollars for miscellaneous charges you expected to be included in the hourly fee.

It is extremely important to ask the lawyer what the fees will be after your death to "settle" the estate or plan. It is quite common to be charged a reasonable amount—$500 to $1,500—for preparing the will or trust, only to find that when you die, the lawyer charges a percentage of the estate to "settle the estate" after death. It's not unusual for a lawyer to charge 1 to 1½ percent of the fair market value of the assets to settle the estate, and another 1 to 1½ percent of the fair market value of the assets to prepare the federal death tax return, if one is required. Add up the value of your assets and compute the cost!

It is possible to find a lawyer who charges a flat fee to prepare your documents but will charge an hourly fee to settle the estate after you are gone. This is typically more cost-efficient.

QUESTION?

Should you ask for a confirmation?
Yes. The lawyer should put his or her estimate in writing and confirm the services that will be provided. Also, ask the lawyer to confirm, in writing, the maximum amount you can expect to be billed.

Paying in Advance

Many lawyers ask for what is called a *retainer.* This is an amount of money the lawyer requests be placed on deposit before he or she starts the job. You should not have to pay for all of the services in advance, only a portion of the estimated cost. It is common to pay a retainer in advance, but it is also possible to find a lawyer who will not bill until the job is done. This really depends on the billing practice of the lawyer or law firm. It does not mean the lawyer is bad or evil merely because he or she requests money in advance.

Chapter 3

The Five Steps of Creating a Plan

Sometimes you don't start a project such as estate planning because it seems overwhelming. It is easier to approach any challenge if you have step-by-step instructions. Creating a plan for your family and loved ones is a five-step process that you needn't fear.

Step One: Learn the Rules

Learning the rules can be fun if you have the right attitude. However, most don't view this as fun; rather they see it as a chore to do when they are ready to die. But what these people don't realize is that they are actually doing estate planning every day.

You make decisions all the time about where you are going to work, how much money you make, how you spend your money, and how your money makes you and your family happy. As you make your daily decisions, you are probably thinking about what your children are going to do when they grow up. You may be considering how you are going to save money to help your children with college or assist them with their career choices. At the same time, you are planning for your own retirement. When you make everyday decisions for yourself and your family, you are engaged in the process of estate planning. As you will see, there is more to estate planning than making your final decisions.

Several Options Available

When you learn the rules about probate, wills, trusts, joint property, and taxes, you are working on a plan that will continue after you are gone. While you are doing your everyday planning, start thinking about how you would want your property managed for the benefit of your family if you were gone. You may decide that if something happened to you, it would be best to have your property distributed as soon as possible to your spouse. If this is your plan, you may choose a simple will, or upon further research, you may decide that joint property is the best plan.

If you have young children, you may think about who would manage your property and money for your children if something happened to you and your spouse. As you've learned, you can name a guardian for your minor children, but you may decide that the person you've chosen to raise your children isn't the best person to oversee their financial property. In which case, you could name one person to physically take care of your children and a different person to manage your children's money and property.

Perhaps during the planning process you discover that your family would need more money if something happened to you. This may lead you to investigate some life insurance to provide for their security. As you can see, one thing often leads to another. It helps to know the rules and be aware of all the options available to you.

ALERT!

If you are concerned about who would manage your property and money for your children if something happened to you, you should consider creating a revocable trust. A revocable trust allows you to name a trustee who will manage your property according to the instructions you put in your trust document.

Life Is Like Monopoly

Planning is like playing the game of Monopoly. Your life is like a Monopoly game board. Every year you travel around the board. You buy properties that make sense for you. You probably play the game differently than your neighbor or even the other members of your family. We all make different choices about the same things. You might like the steady income stream of properties like the railroad properties. Or perhaps you want to buy one piece of expensive property and build on it. But like the game of Monopoly, life has chance cards. You don't know when you are going to land on that chance card, or what that card is going to make you do.

When you play Monopoly there are other players. Your family is like the other players in the game. If you quit the game, the other players can understand how you played and are more prepared to play the game without you.

Estate planning is a dynamic process. It can be exciting to learn the rules and keep your plan current and ready. It's important to learn about all the options available to you before setting forth with one specific legal document or estate plan. In the following chapters, you will learn everything you need to know about your options. It's a good idea to keep a pencil handy. You may want to jot down notes on each, naming the advantages and disadvantages, as well as how it may fit in with your family's needs.

Step Two: Organize Your Assets

It is important to keep the information about your property and the debts you owe current. If you are organized, you will be able to have a plan in place that is ready for your family. You will be able to save money now as well as save your family an enormous amount of money if something happened to you.

Organizational System

Chapter 2 recommended that you develop a system to organize the information about your property. In your three-ring binder or notebook, you should have a separate piece of paper for each property you own. Each property should include information such as the value of the property, what you paid for it, the cost of any improvements you made, the debt against the property, and how it is owned. When you organize the information and keep it current, it will help you make the best choices while you are alive. It will also allow you to evaluate all of your property together and to have a plan in place should you pass on. It's best to review your plan on an annual basis.

You should think about each piece of property you own from two perspectives: whether you are currently making the best choices about that piece of property and what would happen to that property if you were gone.

Evaluating the Information Gathered

Evaluating the information about each piece of property you own can reap tremendous benefits for you now, as well as after you are gone. For example, assume that you have a piece of paper that describes your car. If you think about the costs associated with your car, you might take the time to evaluate whether you are paying too much for insurance. Shop around! You might save money by keeping track of when your car has been serviced—tires, oil change, brakes, etc. And of course, you can plan for what you want to happen to your car if you are gone.

You might discover that you owe more on your car than the car is currently worth. Or, if you lease your car, you may discover that your family would owe money on the lease if something happened to you. These discoveries might lead you to make choices now about your property, as well as what will happen to your property when you are gone.

Let's say you have a sheet of paper that describes your home. One of the pieces of information about your home would be how much you owe and the interest rate you are paying on any loans against it. When you are organizing your notebook for your estate plan, you should evaluate the interest rate you are currently paying. If there are interest rates available that are less than when you financed your home, you may find you can save money now by refinancing your home. And of course, while you are evaluating all of the current costs associated with your home, you can decide who would receive your home if you were gone and whether he or she could afford to maintain it.

FACT

If you can drop your interest rate by 1 percent on a thirty-year mortgage, this saves you $69 per month for every $100,000 of debt. If you owe $200,000 on your home and you can drop your interest rate by 1 percent, you will save $138 per month! Exact savings can vary depending on compounding.

If you have life insurance, describe the attributes of the life insurance on a piece of paper. You may discover that there are new life insurance products available that will pay a larger death benefit for lower annual premiums. This can help you now with the cash flow. And you can also evaluate who will receive the life insurance benefits when you are gone. You may discover that your life insurance will cause your estate to owe federal death taxes. You will learn how to make changes to your plan to avoid any federal death taxes on your life insurance.

Planning Inventory

You may not be the notebook type of person. Or you may feel that you do not need to organize your assets this way to create a plan that meets your needs. Another way to get organized is to complete a planning inventory. A planning inventory is a form that gathers the information you need to evaluate the property you own, assesses whether your estate would be subject to federal death taxes, and prepares you to create the documents you need. A sample inventory is included in Appendix C. The inventory guides you through the steps to gather the information you need to plan, and it also brings all of the information together in one place for your family to access easily if something happens to you. Take a moment and review the information requested by the inventory.

ALERT!

If you do not organize the information about your property either by filling out an inventory or preparing a three-ring binder or notebook, your family probably will not know how to find the needed information.

When something happens to you, your family is full of grief. It is heart-wrenching for your family to have to go through all of your papers trying to gather the needed information. You can avoid this crisis for your family by being prepared. Sometimes even when a person chooses to organize the information in a three-ring notebook, they like to also complete the inventory, because the inventory summarizes the information in the notebook.

Step Three: Decide Who, What, and When

An old journalism adage applies here: You get the right story when you tell who, what, where, when, and why. Your family is a story. It is a story that changes all the time. Who are your loved ones? What are your goals for them? Where are your loved ones living? When would you want your loved ones to receive your property and why? Get ready to tell your story.

Think about your notebook. If you haven't already, take out a separate piece of paper and write down the name of every person you would include in your plan. Then begin to ask yourself what that person is currently doing. Which piece of property or properties would you like that person to have? Put the piece of paper that describes that property under the piece of paper describing the person to whom you would leave that property. Develop little stacks of paper under each person's name. Then when you look at the stacks, you can ask the next question. When would you like that person to receive the property? You might find yourself beginning to think about things like:

- Would that person be able to take care of the property if something happened to you tomorrow?
- Would it promote maturity if that person received the property tomorrow?
- Would it be better if that person received the property later in life?
- If something happens to you, should the property be sold?
- How much income tax or death tax would it cost if you leave that piece of property to the named person?
- Is your plan fair?

When you think about your property and the persons who would enjoy your property if something were to happen to you, you may discover that the goals you have now for your loved ones and family are very different from the goals you had ten years ago.

You need to look at your plan to see if it meets your family's needs today and re-evaluate it regularly. The answers to the questions who, what, and when will change over time. And since you don't know when something might happen to you, it's best to try to keep up with changing times.

Most people do not keep their plans current because they don't understand the planning tools that are available or how they work. They don't know how to change their plan to meet the changing needs of their family. And last but not least, they don't want to spend a lot of money keeping their plan current every year.

ALERT!

Your plans and goals change over time, so don't prepare a will or trust and hide it safely away to be forgotten. Be sure to keep your plan current with the changing needs of your family.

The beauty of learning the rules is that it allows you to do most of the work. Many times, you can make the necessary changes yourself, without the help of a lawyer. But even if you do need the help of a lawyer, when you understand the planning tools available and how they work, it will be much less expensive for you to have your plan tweaked.

Step Four: Choose Your Planning Tools

There are so many fun planning tools available. When you understand your options and how the planning tools work, you can become an involved player in your plan rather than a passive observer. It is always scary to have someone tell you what you need to do, without explaining why you should do that particular thing. In the same way, it can be disturbing when you don't understand the planning tools or what the consequences will be if you don't plan. When something scares you, it's natural to try to avoid it.

You don't need to be nervous and scared. And there's certainly no reason to avoid these planning tools. You simply need to figure out how they can work for you. Once you do, you suddenly don't have to be a passive participant in planning for your family. You can make decisions that may help you save money now and provide for the security of your loved ones later.

Planning Tools Available

There are numerous planning tools available. You will soon learn the rules regarding:

- Wills
- Retirement plans
- Life insurance
- Joint property
- Trusts
- Annuities
- Taxes

One Tool Affects Another

You will probably have or need more than one planning tool. When you create anything, there are typically parts that are combined to make a whole finished product. When you make a decision about one planning tool, it may change what you do with another planning tool. For instance, let's say you have an IRA, and you learn how the IRA is taxed when you die. You aren't happy with this outcome so you conduct more research. What you find allows you to change some of your IRA elections to reduce the tax impact.

Or perhaps you already have a will in place, but you learn that it has no impact on how or to whom your insurance, annuities, IRA, and joint property are paid and distributed. You might have thought that if you put instructions in your will about how these items were to be distributed, that your will would control. As you now know, this isn't true, so you will probably want to re-evaluate your plan to make it coincide with your wishes.

Most families have different types of property and need multiple planning tools to accomplish their goals. When you understand what each of the planning tools can do for you, you will be in a position to play the game, participate in the choices, and create a plan that you can maintain and change as the needs of your family change.

ALERT!

Every person should have a will or trust. Even if all of your property is in joint name with your spouse, you should have a document that will direct how your property passes in the unlikely event that both you and your spouse die in a common accident.

Step Five: Implement Your Plan

A plan is no good unless you take the steps that are necessary to implement it. Many people sit around and think about plans, but don't do anything to set them in motion. This failure to implement a plan is even more common with estate planning. The reason is that most plans you make result in something you look forward to. Let's face it, it's unlikely that there are people out there who jump out of bed in the morning and say, "I can't wait to do my estate planning today, because I'm really looking forward to passing on!" But when you think about estate planning as part of your everyday life and consider the benefits you can enjoy today by creating and implementing a plan, you may have a little more motivation to get started.

ESSENTIAL

A good estate plan is not set in motion in one hour. It's probably not accomplished in one day or even one week. In order to implement a plan, you need to be organized, understand your options and planning tools, and think about how your property should be distributed or managed if you are gone. This all takes time and effort.

If you follow the steps recommended in this book, you will be well prepared to implement your plan. Implementing your plan is not about having a lawyer draft documents. It is about knowing your story—who, what, where, when, and why. When you understand your story, you can walk through the steps to determine which planning tools meet your needs. Then, you can either prepare the necessary documents yourself, or you can make an appointment with a lawyer who will be able to draft the documents for you. And remember, your plan will probably change regularly, as your needs and the needs of your family change. (E)

Chapter 4

Understanding the Probate Process

If you stopped several people on the street and asked, "What is probate?" the majority of people would respond, "Probate is what happens when a person dies." You are going to learn in this chapter that this is not an accurate statement.

Why an Estate Needs to Be Probated

You may think that probate happens automatically. However, there is no arm of government that starts the probate process when you die. There aren't even any probate police. Probate is like a lawsuit. Someone has to file papers with the probate court in the county where you die to start the process. The best way to understand probate is to learn why an estate needs to be probated. There are four reasons:

- You owned property in your individual name.
- You had unpaid bills and debts that are not paid by your survivors.
- There is a dispute about how your property will be distributed.
- You died with a minor child or children and there is no surviving natural parent.

Property Owned in Your Individual Name

If you own property that was titled in your individual name, such as real estate, stocks, bonds, cars, boats, etc., and you die, there needs to be someone who can sign your name after you are gone to transfer the title from your name to someone else's. If you had a checking account, a savings account, or some other financial account in your individual name, there must be someone who can sign your checks or withdraw money after you are gone. The only person who is legally authorized to sign for you is your executor. (In some states the executor is called a personal representative.) An executor is the person you name in your will to carry out the instructions contained in the will. If you do not have a will, the probate court will name an executor.

FACT

If you own property in joint name with someone else when you die, your loved ones will not need an executor to sign, because the title will pass automatically to the surviving joint tenant.

The Creditors

The second reason an estate might need to be probated is to pay your bills and debts after you are gone. The persons or entities to whom you owe money, such as the bank for the mortgage on your house or the debt on your car or credit card companies, are called *creditors*. If your creditors are not paid after you die, they are entitled to file papers with the probate court to open a proceeding if your survivors have not already done so. If your loved ones have already opened a probate proceeding, the unpaid creditors will file a claim seeking an order to be paid. If all of your bills and debts are paid after you are gone, there will be no creditors who can open a probate proceeding or file a claim to be paid.

Disagreements Over Distribution

The third reason your estate might be probated is because your heirs and loved ones disagree on how to distribute your property after you are gone. If your family disagrees, one or more members of your family are entitled to file a petition with the probate court to resolve the dispute. When this happens, the probate court judge will typically order your property sold and the proceeds from the sale of your property will be distributed to your family.

ALERT!

When there is a dispute about how to divide your property after you are gone, each person who disagrees needs to hire a lawyer to represent his or her interest in the probate court proceeding. At $175 to $200 per hour, imagine how expensive this can be!

Naming a Legal Guardian

The final reason there might need to be a probate proceeding is if you died with a minor child or children and there is no surviving natural parent. Then there must be a probate proceeding to name a legal guardian for your minor child or children. If you have a will that names a legal guardian, unless there is an objection to the person named, the court will enter an order naming that person as legal guardian. If you don't have a will, the court will hear testimony on who is best suited to serve as the legal guardian. It does not matter whether you do or do not have a will, there will always be a probate proceeding when you die with a minor child or children if there is no surviving parent.

Property That Is Not Subject to Probate

Property that is titled in your individual name must be probated when you are gone, because you are not available to sign your name to transfer the title to your family. The easiest way to understand this concept is to learn what property is *not* subject to probate.

The following property is not subject to probate:

- Property you owned in joint name with another person or persons
- Life insurance proceeds, as long as the estate is not named beneficiary
- Annuities, as long as the estate is not named beneficiary
- IRAs, as long as the estate is not named beneficiary
- Other retirement plans, as long as the estate is not named beneficiary
- Assets held in trust, as long as the estate is not named beneficiary of the trust

These properties are not subject to probate even if you have a will because they either pass automatically to a surviving joint tenant or the property is distributed according to a beneficiary election you made while you were alive.

If your property is owned in joint name with at least one surviving joint tenant; your property is held in trust; or you have life insurance, retirement accounts, or annuities, there is no property that is subject to probate. If your creditors are paid and you have no minor children, there will be no probate.

It is a good idea to have every company with whom you have insurance, retirement accounts, or annuities send you a confirmation of your beneficiary election. These choices could have been made many years ago.

The Probate Proceeding

There is a lengthy and very formal process that must be followed in each state to probate an estate. Contrary to popular belief, if a person dies with a will, probate is still necessary. The typical steps in a probate proceeding are:

1. A petition is filed with your local probate court to start the probate process.
2. The probate court issues an order naming an executor.
3. A notice of death is published in the local newspaper.
4. Bills and debts must be paid.
5. Your property must be valued.
6. Your property is distributed.
7. Accountings and inventories must be filed with the probate court.
8. Papers are filed to close the estate.

Who Files the Petition?

If you have a will, it almost always names an executor. However, the person named in the will does not become the executor automatically. This person must petition the probate court seeking appointment as executor. The probate court judge will review your will and the petition to determine if the will has been signed with the proper formalities, and then determine if the person seeking appointment as executor is qualified to serve. If so, the judge will enter an order appointing the person as executor. This opens the probate process. It is the order appointing the person as executor that gives her or him the legal authority to sign documents for you when you are gone.

If there is no will or the person named in your will is not available, the probate court will determine who should serve. Each state has laws that establish the priority of who should be named as executor in such cases. Typically, the surviving spouse is given first priority and then the children. When there is no surviving spouse, it is not uncommon for the surviving children to disagree about who should serve. When this happens, the probate court will schedule a hearing and hear testimony about who is best qualified to serve. That's when things really start getting expensive. Imagine that there are two surviving children, each of whom feels he or she should serve as executor. If they can't agree on who will serve, each will file a petition seeking appointment. Both children will need their own lawyer.

FACT

Some states allow the judge to review the petition and enter an order without a hearing. Other states require the judge to take testimony from the persons who witnessed your will. Sometimes a relative or an interested person might file a contest with the probate court objecting either to the validity of your will or to the appointment of the person named in your will to serve as executor.

After the Executor Is Appointed

After the executor is appointed, the estate places a notice in your local newspaper, providing the name of the person who died, the name of the executor, and an address where the executor can be contacted. Usually the estate posts the address of the lawyer who is representing the estate as the contact. Once the notice is published in the local newspaper, most state laws require the estate to wait three to six months before distributing the assets. This waiting period gives all of the creditors who have not been paid an opportunity to submit their bills to your estate and also allows anyone who thinks they have an interest in your property an opportunity to file a claim. This waiting period creates a substantial delay for your loved ones and costs more money.

The probate proceeding for your estate could possibly be closed within six months as long as no one:

- Contests the validity of your will
- Argues that you were not competent to make a will
- Objects to the appointment of the executor
- Files a claim against the estate
- Disagrees about the valuation of the property
- Contests how your property will be distributed

Probate Takes Time

The length of time it takes to probate an estate depends on the amount of time it takes your family to gather the necessary information, the number of months your state requires the estate to wait after posting the legal notice in the local newspaper, and whether or not anyone files a contest or a claim.

Your family has time. The only task that needs to be done quickly after you are gone, if you had a will, is the filing of the original within a certain period of time with the probate court in the county where you died. The time period typically ranges from within ten to thirty days of the date of death. Your family can file the will with the local probate court themselves. Once this is done, your family has time to shop for a lawyer.

There may be a rush to open probate if there are no funds that can be accessed to pay bills because all of the accounts were in your individual name. Then your family will need to have an executor appointed as quickly as possible, since the executor will be able to access the money.

No Less Than Six Months

If everything goes perfectly, the probate process will take at least six months. Your family will typically spend the first week handling the burial or cremation arrangements. Then your family will make an appointment with a lawyer. The lawyer will get enough information to prepare the petition to start the probate process and will provide your family with a list of needed information.

It usually takes the probate court judge one week to review the petition and sign an order appointing the executor. The executor might be appointed within one week if you live in a state that allows the judge to issue an order without a hearing. If a hearing is required, it might be several more weeks before the judge signs an order appointing the executor. If someone contests the appointment of the executor, further hearings will be needed to determine who will serve as the permanent executor. Most states then require at least a three-month waiting period after the legal posting is made in the local newspaper. Some states require a six-month waiting period.

The lawyer must file all state and federal tax returns, including a final income tax return. However, the information may not be available to file the final income tax return until after January 31 of the year following the death. This increases the delay. Lastly, the lawyer must prepare final inventories and accountings to close the estate.

Probate Protects

The probate process is very old-fashioned. It requires a lot of formalities to try to protect your family against the possibility that your property would be improperly distributed after you are gone. The probate system also protects unpaid creditors. These protections create cost and delay. However, you are going to learn that there are steps you can take and documents you can prepare to avoid the probate process and save your family time, money, and frustration.

Probate Usually Requires a Lawyer

If your family needs to probate your estate, they will likely need to hire a lawyer. It is very difficult to file the necessary papers with the probate court without the assistance of a legal professional. Your family can get the paperwork they need directly from the probate court in the county where you died. However, the employees who work at the probate court are not allowed to give legal advice. Therefore, they usually won't tell you what forms you need, and they can't help you fill out the forms even if you know what forms to ask for.

The time your lawyer needs to spend preparing the paperwork to probate your estate will be substantially reduced if you do your homework while you are alive and your family understands the probate process. If you prepared a notebook containing all of the information about your family and your assets, and it contains a copy of your will, as well as a copy of all of the paperwork recommended in Chapter 2, you will have saved the lawyer hours of work.

If you stay organized and you keep your plan updated, you will be able to be more specific about how your property should be distributed. This reduces the possibility that someone will contest your choice of an executor or disagree about what you want done with your property. It will also keep the information current about the bills you owe. If your creditors are paid, they can't file a claim against your estate causing more expense and delay for your family.

ALERT!

It is almost impossible for your family to work their way through the probate process without hiring a lawyer. However, when your family is prepared, the cost of the probate process will be reduced dramatically.

The Cost of Probate

Most lawyers charge a minimum fee, plus a percentage of the total value of the property, to probate an estate. A typical fee is $1,500 for the first $100,000 of property plus 1 percent of the value of the assets above $100,000. For example, if the value of the property you own when you die equals $400,000, a typical fee would be $4,500—$1,500 plus 1 percent times $300,000.

It is possible to find a lawyer who will charge by the hour. If your loved ones are prepared and understand the basic steps of the probate process, it is typically cheaper to hire a lawyer who charges by the hour. If you hire a lawyer to prepare your will, you should ask the lawyer how he or she bills to probate the estate when you are gone. If you are not satisfied with the answer, you may want to have a different lawyer prepare your will.

Meeting with a Lawyer

When your family meets with a lawyer following your death, they should bring the information contained in your notebook. If you did not prepare a notebook, your family should provide the following information.

- The legal name, address, social security number, and birth date of every person named in the will
- If there is no will, the legal names, addresses, social security numbers, and birth dates of the spouse and children—if there is no spouse or children, the names, addresses, social security numbers, and birth dates of the parents and brothers and sisters
- A copy of the death certificate
- Driver's license and voter registration of the person who died
- All of the credit cards in the sole name of the person who died
- Health insurance information
- A copy of the title for everything that the person owned in his or her individual name (This would include the title to any real estate, cars, boats, or motorcycles.)
- A copy of the most recent statement for all bank accounts and brokerage accounts
- A list of all of the retirement accounts
- All life insurance policies or annuities
- A list of all of debts

ESSENTIAL

The best way to organize the information is to go to the office supply store and buy a box of manila folders. Put each piece of information in a separate manila folder and label the folder. Then, prepare a table of contents describing the information you have gathered.

Your family is now ready to shop for a lawyer to probate your estate. Price-shopping is very important! Lawyers spend a lot of time explaining the rules about the probate process and helping your family find the information needed to probate your estate. If the lawyer knows that your family is prepared and has a good idea of what needs to be done, he or she will give your family a better price. Time is money. If your family is prepared, they will likely save thousand of dollars in legal fees. (E)

Chapter 5

How to
Avoid Probate

If you did not own any property in your individual name, your bills are paid, no one objects to how your property is distributed, and there are no minor children without a surviving parent, your loved ones can avoid the probate process. It takes some planning while you are alive, but it is not difficult to save your family this hassle.

Reasons for Avoiding the Probate Process

The simplest reason to avoid the probate process is to save your loved ones the inevitable cost and delay. The probate process exists to protect your assets when you are gone. Imagine what might happen if anyone could sign your name to transfer title of your property. When you own property in your name when you die, the probate process requires that an executor be appointed, who, under the supervision of the probate court, can transfer your property according to the terms contained in your will or according to the laws established in your state if you do not have a will. While these protections work for your best interests, they do cost time and money.

You can avoid these costs and delays by structuring the ownership of your property in a way that will avoid the probate process. When you avoid the probate process by managing how your assets are owned, you also reduce the possibility of conflict among your loved ones when you are gone.

ESSENTIAL

By organizing your assets and liabilities and developing a plan for your loved ones, you can easily avoid the probate process. You may find the process of developing a plan allows you to analyze the property you own and helps you make decisions about your property that will let you enjoy the benefits while you are alive.

The only time probate is absolutely necessary is if you die survived by a minor child or children and the other parent is also gone. Then, probate must occur to appoint a legal guardian for the minor child or children. If there are no minor children involved, then you can easily avoid the probate process for your loved ones through the use of one or more of the following plans:

- Joint property
- Trusts
- Life insurance

- Retirement plans
- Annuities

The choices you make will depend on the type of plan you want to craft for your family. Planning for your loved ones while you are living is a game, and it can be fun when you know the rules. Think of it as a big puzzle. There are several pieces you have to work with, but you win only when you figure out how the pieces fit together to create the perfect whole, or plan.

Titling Property

There are a number of ways you can own your property that will avoid the probate process when you are gone:

- Your property can be owned in joint name with another person.
- Your property can be owned in trust.
- Your property can pass by contract and not by your will.

Joint Tenancy

The easiest way to avoid the probate process is to own property in joint name with another person. This is technically known as holding property in joint tenancy. If your property is owned in joint tenancy with another person, when you die, title passes automatically to the surviving joint tenant and probate is avoided. It is very common for a husband and wife to own property in joint name. When the first spouse dies, the property belongs to the surviving spouse, because the surviving spouse was a joint tenant.

FACT

It is not very common for a husband and wife to die in the same accident. Therefore, owning all of your property in joint name with your spouse is a "cheap" estate plan. Title will pass automatically to the surviving spouse, and there will be no need for her or him to probate the estate.

There are two factors you should consider prior to placing all of your property in joint name with your spouse. First, you and your spouse could die in a common accident. If this were to happen, the property would need to be probated because there would be no surviving owner. Second, there can be negative income tax consequences to owning your property in joint name with your spouse.

Multiple Joint Tenants

You can have a will as a backup to provide instructions on how to distribute your property if you and your spouse die in a common accident. Another way to protect against that risk is to add other joint tenants to your property. There is no limit to the number of persons who can own a piece of property as joint tenants. If you add your children as joint tenants, and you and your spouse die, then your property will automatically be owned by your children.

This may sound like a good idea, but there are practical reasons why you and your spouse might not want to do this. When you add someone as a joint tenant to most types of property, you are making a gift of a portion of the property to that joint tenant. For example, assume you have two children, and you and your spouse decide to add both as joint tenants on the deed to your home. When you do this, you are making a gift to the children. Depending on the value of the property, this may generate a gift tax to you and your spouse.

ALERT!

Owning property in joint name with another person or a number of persons is a simple way for the surviving joint tenant or tenants to avoid the probate process. But beware, joint ownership may not accomplish the family objectives.

If you and your spouse decide to sell the property after you have added your two children as joint tenants, half of the sale proceeds must be paid to the children, since they own half of your property. You also can't change your mind. You have given half of the property to your children. If you want the property back, the children don't have to give it to you.

Unexpected Results

There are several other things you should consider before you add other people as joint tenants to your property. Joint tenancy can have unexpected results. For example, if you add your two children as joint tenants to your property and one of them dies in a common accident with you, the property will belong to your one surviving child. The child who died with you may be survived by her or his own children. If you had wanted those grandchildren to share the property, it will not happen.

When you own property in joint name with your spouse, there is a negative income tax consequence to your surviving spouse. When you own property in joint name with someone other than your spouse, the income tax consequences may or may not be negative, depending on your circumstances. There are also estate and gift tax consequences to owning property in joint name. While these rules are carefully covered in Chapter 10, you need to be aware of the possibilities now before you jump into a joint tenancy. Be sure to thoroughly research all options and consequences before making any final decisions.

Place Property in Trust

If you create a trust for your family, the property owned by the trust will avoid the probate process. Frankly, many of the disadvantages of owning property in joint name are avoided when the property is owned by a trust. If you understand the history of trusts, it will help you understand how a property held in trust will avoid the probate process.

History of Trusts

The basics of trust law have remained unchanged for centuries. Trusts evolved from early English law. In England, no one could own property except for the king. The workers became very dissatisfied with doing all of the work and not owning the land. As the discontent mounted, the king granted the workers use of the land, though the legal title remained with him. Eventually the workers were allowed to hand down the use of the property to their heirs. It became the law in England that the king held legal title of the property for the benefit of the workers, who held equitable title. The separation of legal title from equitable title is the foundation of our trust law.

A trust is a way for you to name someone who will hold legal title to your property for the benefit of your loved ones. The person who holds the title is known as the trustee, and your loved ones, who will enjoy the use of the property, are known as your beneficiaries.

FACT

The beauty of a trust is that while you are living you serve as the settlor or grantor of the trust and define all of the rights. You can also serve as trustee of the trust, which means you hold legal title. You can also be the beneficiary of the trust while you are living. You truly enjoy all of the benefits of property ownership.

When you create a trust, you decide what rights your beneficiaries will have. You are known as the *settlor* or *grantor* of the trust. In that capacity you will name a trustee. The trustee is like the king. The trustee holds legal title to the property for the benefit of the beneficiaries. The beneficiaries are like the workers: They hold equitable title to the property and enjoy the benefits you gave them in the trust document you created.

You Make All the Decisions

When you die, the trust document you created names a person or an entity to serve as trustee when you are gone. This is technically known as a *successor trustee*. Also, as creator, or settlor, of the trust, you name the persons who will enjoy the benefits of the property when you are gone. These are known as *successor beneficiaries*. The trust document you create will provide the successor trustee very detailed instructions on what to do with the property. Those instructions govern who will enjoy your property, when they will enjoy the property, and how they will enjoy the property.

This is why property that is held in trust avoids the probate process. You own the property while you are living, but you own it in your legal capacity as a trustee. When you die, whomever you named as successor trustee automatically becomes the legal owner of the property. The rules about trusts are covered in detail in Chapters 11 through 14. But, for now, just understand why property held in trust avoids the probate process.

FACT

There are certain types of property that are not subject to probate because the property is governed by an agreement you entered into while you were living. This type of property will be distributed according to the terms of the contract, and will not be affected by whether or not you have a will.

Make Good Use of Life Insurance

When you apply for life insurance, the application asks you who will receive the life insurance benefits when you die. You can name one or more persons as the beneficiary. When you name more than one person to receive the policy benefit, you also decide what percentage of the proceeds each person will receive.

Your will has absolutely no effect on who will receive the proceeds from your life insurance policies. As a matter of fact, your will could specifically say, "I leave all of my life insurance to my children, in equal shares," but this clause would be disregarded completely, and the policy proceeds would be paid to the person or persons you named when you bought the life insurance.

Payable to the Estate

However, there are two ways that your will can affect how your life insurance proceeds will be paid. The first is if you named your estate as ~~probated~~ the beneficiary when you bought the life insurance policy. Then the life insurance proceeds will be paid to your estate and distributed according to the terms of your will. You might name your estate as beneficiary of your life insurance policy if you couldn't decide on a person. Sometimes when a young person is starting a new job and his or her employer pays for a life insurance policy as part of the employee benefit package, the new employee does not know whom he or she wants to name as beneficiary. In that case, it is typical just to check the box "payable to my estate."

ALERT!

It is not always a good idea to name your estate as beneficiary of your life insurance policy, because the life insurance proceeds will need to be probated before they can be distributed.

When the Beneficiary Is No Longer Living

The second way your will could affect how your life insurance proceeds are paid is if the person or persons you name to receive the life insurance proceeds are not alive. Then, the insurance company will pay the policy proceeds to your estate. Your will may not reference the insurance because it was supposed to be paid directly to the person or persons named in the policy. But most wills have a clause that says, "Distribute any remaining property I own to X," and the insurance proceeds would be distributed accordingly.

Life insurance proceeds avoid the probate process. But before you close the book on what you need to know about life insurance, you should read Chapter 15 to make sure your family does not pay unnecessary death taxes.

Consider Creating Retirement Accounts

IRAs, Roth IRAs, and employer-provided retirement accounts are like life insurance. The retirement benefits are paid to the beneficiary or beneficiaries you named when you opened the retirement account or completed the paperwork with your employer.

It is irrelevant what your will says. The only way your retirement benefits will be governed by your will is if you named the estate as the beneficiary of your retirement benefits or the person or persons you named are not alive. Then your retirement benefits will be paid to your estate and will need to be probated.

Although life insurance proceeds and retirement accounts are alike because the proceeds avoid the probate process, the income tax consequences of each are completely different. The rules regarding the federal death taxes associated with retirement accounts and the income tax consequences to your beneficiaries are covered in Chapter 17.

ALERT!

It is very important to double-check who you have named as beneficiary of your life insurance policies and your retirement accounts. The beneficiary you named initially may not be who you want today to receive the benefits at your death.

Annuities May Be the Answer

Annuities are like life insurance and retirement accounts. Annuities are paid to the person or persons you named in the application when you purchased the annuity. These persons are known as the beneficiaries. Your will does not affect who will receive the annuity benefits unless you named your estate as the beneficiary of your annuity or the person or persons you named as beneficiaries are not living when you die. (Chapter 16 will discuss annuities in further detail.)

Because life insurance, retirement accounts, and annuities are paid to the person or persons you name as beneficiaries, it is important that you obtain a copy of your beneficiary election forms. You would be surprised how many times the beneficiary elections are not what you thought they were. This could be because you forgot who you named, or the information was improperly recorded by the company.

Chapter 6

The Parts of a Will

A will is the legal document that pro-vides instructions on how property that is titled in your name will be distrib-uted when you are gone. Each part of your will serves a different purpose. Once you understand the parts, you can make the decisions needed to begin a draft of your will.

An Overview

A will is a piece of paper that is presented to the probate court after you are gone. The probate court judge needs to be able to read that piece of paper and determine that it is in fact your will and that you signed that will. The judge then issues a court order to distribute your property per your instructions. This all sounds very simple. However, you are not available to testify that the will is in fact yours. The judge has to make sure that no one changed your will without your permission. The judge also needs to determine by reading the will who you wanted to receive your property and what you wanted each person to have. All of these decisions are made without the testimony of the one and only person who really knew what he or she wanted: you! Therefore, your will must speak for itself.

A Will Is Divided into Parts

The more specific you are about what you want, the easier it will be for the probate court judge to make the right decisions about your property. Each part of your will is designed to help the probate court judge interpret your intentions. A will has parts, often referred to as the *articles*. Each article is designed to accomplish a purpose.

Don't Be Intimidated by Fancy Words

Words are intimidating when you don't understand what they mean. For instance, let's say you take your car to a mechanic. The mechanic starts talking about the lifters, pistons, plugs, serpentine belt, and catalytic converter, and you become nervous because you have no idea what he or she is talking about. When your will includes phrases like "descendants by right of representations" or "property passing per stirpes," that same sense of panic fills your body. Don't be intimidated! When you finish reading this chapter, you will understand those fancy words.

FACT

The words in a will are confusing because the law on wills came from our English heritage. Unlike most areas of law where more modern terms have been incorporated into the law, the terminology associated with wills has not changed much for centuries.

Declarations

The first part, or Article I, of your will identifies you and your heirs. This part is referred to as the declaration section. An heir is any person who would receive your property if you died without a will. If you think about a ladder, it will help you understand the heirs you should list in this first part. If you have living heirs at the first step of the ladder, you don't need to go to the second step. If you have no heirs at the first or second step, you need to list your heirs at the third step.

The Ladder of Heirs

The first step, or level, of heirs is your spouse and your children. If you have no spouse, the only heirs at this first step are your children. If one or more of your children have died and are survived by one or more children, the child or children of the child who is gone is included as an heir on the first step of the ladder. If any of these persons are living, you can stop here.

If there is no one living at the first step, you must go to the second step, which includes your mother and father. If your mother is gone, your father is your only heir, and vice versa. If your mother and/or father are living, you can stop. If your mother and father are gone, go to the next step.

The third step is your siblings or their children. If one of your siblings is gone, the child or children of the deceased sibling will become heirs, and should be listed. If you have no spouse, children, grandchildren, parents, brothers, sisters, or children of siblings, you need help from a lawyer to define your heirs. Most people identify or declare the names of their spouse and children.

It may seem silly to spend so much time teaching you about your heirs, but the probate court judge wants to be sure that you knew who your heirs were. Then, if you decide not to leave any property to an heir, later in your will you can explain why you have excluded that heir.

ALERT!

Remember, the probate court judge's job is to issue an order to distribute your property to the persons you name in your will. If you don't identify your heirs in the declaration portion of your will, you run the risk that an excluded heir will contest your will, alleging that you forgot about him or her.

Defining Children

The next part of the declaration section of your will defines the words *child, children,* and *descendants.* The most important thing for you to understand is that the word child (or children) will not include stepchildren or foster children. If you want to make a distribution to a stepchild or a foster child you can do so in Articles III or IV, but you will need to be very specific. As you read on about how to distribute your property, you will learn about the significance of the word *descendant.*

Payment of Debts

The next part of your will, Article II, directs that all of your debts, obligations, and taxes be paid. Any person or entity to which you owed money when you died is called a creditor. You've learned that when you die, one of the first jobs of the executor is to hire a lawyer to file the necessary papers with the probate court. The lawyer will also tell the executor what he or she needs to do to administer your estate. One of the jobs of your executor is to pay the debts and obligations you owed when you died.

If your executor does not pay the creditors, an unpaid creditor is allowed to file a claim against your estate demanding payment. If there are not enough assets to pay all of your debts and obligations, there is an ordering process to determine which debts will be paid in full and which debts will either not be paid or will be partially paid.

Secured Debt

There are certain types of debts that are secured. When a debt is secured by property you owned while you are living, that piece of property can be sold to pay the debt. The best example of this type of secured debt is the debt you owe on your home.

When you borrowed money to buy your home, you signed two types of legal papers. The first was a promissory note. The promissory note made you and whoever else signed the promissory note personally liable for the debt. The second type of paper you signed gave the lender, typically your bank, a security interest in your house, known as a mortgage. If you don't make your payments, the lender has two choices. The lender can sue you and whoever else signed on the promissory note, or the lender can take the house back and sell your home under the terms of the mortgage.

ALERT!

Don't forget that your will has no effect on joint property, nor does it have an effect on IRAs, annuities, or life insurance, where someone other than the estate is named as the beneficiary.

Lenders Have Rights When You Die

When you die, if you owed money on a promissory note, secured by a mortgage on your home, the lender typically has the right to demand that the debt be paid in full. Anytime you own property secured by a mortgage, that property can be sold to pay the debt. Lenders typically don't exercise this right as long as someone continues to make the monthly payments.

Article II may include an excerpt such as the following:

> If any property owned by me jointly, or individually, passing under this will or otherwise, shall be encumbered by a mortgage, pledge, security interest, loan, lien, or unpaid taxes, the indebtedness secured by such encumbrance shall not be charged to or paid by my estate but such property shall pass subject to all encumbrances existing at my death.

This language is merely telling your executor that if there is a secured loan against a particular piece of property you owned, the executor is to distribute that property without paying off the loan against the property.

Please understand that these instructions are not binding on the lender. The lender will have the right to be paid in full before the property is distributed to your heirs, if the lender chooses to exercise its rights under the loan documents. A lender may choose to exercise its right to demand that the property be sold if your estate has more debts than it has assets, and the lender is not comfortable that the other person who signed the note, if there is one, is capable of making the payments.

Before you prepare your will it is a good idea to analyze the property you own, the debt against the property, and how that debt is secured. If your family would not have enough money to pay the outstanding bills, you might consider purchasing some life insurance.

Specific Devises

Devise is the term that is used in a will to describe the fact that you are leaving property to someone. The person to whom you devise property is called a *devisee*. When you make a specific devise, you are describing a piece of property and giving specific instructions to give that property to a named person.

Specific Devise of Tangible Personal Property

Tangible personal property is any property other than real estate that you can feel or touch. Tangible property does not include bank accounts, shares of stock, certificates of deposit, bonds, partnership interests, or any other financial interests. These items are known as intangible personal property.

Most wills include a separate article telling the executor what to do with your tangible personal property. For example, let's say a will specifies that all of the tangible personal property is to be left to the spouse, and if the spouse is not living, to the children. If the children cannot agree on how to divide the tangible personal property within six months, the will states that the executor shall decide how to divide the tangible personal property, and the decision of the executor is final and binding.

Even if your will states that the decision of the executor shall be final and binding, someone could file a contest with the probate court, alleging that the executor is breaching his or her duty. It will be tough for that person to win, but it is expensive for your estate to spend money on a lawyer to defend the contest.

Avoiding Conflict

If you think your children or heirs are going to fight about what each one receives, you can specifically describe each piece of tangible personal property and who should receive that property. Heirs typically fight about jewelry, crystal, china, furniture, cars, boats, and collectibles. It takes time and thought on your part to include specifics in your will, but it can avoid hard feelings after you are gone.

Or you might consider putting a clause in your will that says, "If my children can not agree on how to distribute the rest of my tangible personal property within six months after my death, I hereby instruct the executor to sell the disputed items and divide the proceeds equally between my children." It would be almost impossible for any child to contest this language.

Who Pays Expenses

You should include instructions about who pays the expenses incurred in storing, packing, or moving the tangible personal property.

A will may state that these expenses are not to be charged against the devisee who receives the tangible personal property. In plain English this means that if there are expenses in storing, packing, or moving any tangible personal property, those expenses are to be paid from other assets or property in your estate, and are not charged to the one who receives the property. If this is not your intention, you should instruct your executor that any expenses for storing, packing, or moving will be charged against the devisee who receives the property. Sometimes it's not fair if one child lives 3,000 miles away that the other heirs must bear the expense of packing and moving the property!

Specific Devises of Other Property

There is no magic number of how many articles there will be in your will. If you want to make specific devises of any other property, you should have another article titled "Specific Devises of Other Property." You should number each paragraph. In each paragraph you should describe in detail each piece of property and who is going to receive that property. For instance:

1. I leave the property located at 7301 Chase Drive, Sarasota, Florida, to my daughter.
2. I leave my brokerage account held at X Company to my son.
3. I leave the balance of my savings account held at X Bank to my daughter.

FACT

When you leave a specific devise of property to a named individual in your will, make sure that the property you are attempting to leave to the named person is actually titled in your individual name. The property could be very clearly described, but if the property is owned in joint name, the will has no effect.

There are two points you should consider regarding specific devises. First, if you don't own the described property when you die, the devise is ignored, and the devisee does not get other property unless it is already specified. Second, you should specify what happens to the property if the devisee you name is not living. For example, if you leave your daughter 7301 Chase Drive, that provision should continue and state that if your daughter is not living, the property shall pass to her children, or to her brother, or according to the residual clause of your will. These are choices you need to make when you include specific devises in your will.

Per Stirpes

There are two legal terms you should understand. The first is *per stirpes,* and the second is *per capita.* Let's first take a look at per stirpes. Whenever you leave property to a person per stirpes, this has a very definite legal effect. It means that if the named person is dead, the property passes to the lineal descendants, by representation. The best way to understand this concept is with a diagram.

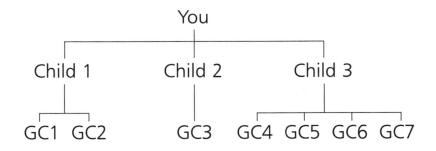

Per stirpes means that if Child 1 is deceased, Child 1's share will be divided equally between GC1 and GC2. In other words, Child 1's $1/3$ share will be divided equally between GC1 and GC2, who will each receive $1/6$ of the property. If you would rather have Child 1's property distributed to your other two children, Child 2 and Child 3, you don't want to use the term *per stirpes.*

Assume that all three of your children are gone. Because you have left the property per stirpes, Child 1's children will each receive $1/6$ ($1/2 \times 1/3$); Child 2's child will receive $1/3$ because Child 2 had only one child; and Child 3's children will each take $1/12$ of the property ($1/4 \times 1/3$).

This may not be what you intended. If your children are all gone, you might want each of the seven grandchildren to take equal shares. In which case you shouldn't use the term per stirpes.

Per Capita

Another option is to use the term *per capita*. If you leave the property to a group per capita, and a member of the group is gone, the property goes in equal shares to the other persons in the group. For instance, if you leave your property per capita to your three children and one child dies, then the property will pass to your two living children, and not to the children of your deceased child.

FACT

If you don't define who will take a property if the specific devisee is gone with the term per stirpes or per capita, you can specifically name who should receive the property and in what share. It makes your will longer, but ensures that your property will pass the way you want.

Residuary Devise

This is the clause that distributes the rest of your property. This may also be the clause that will distribute specifically devised property if the person to whom you specifically devised property is not living, and you put in a provision that reads, "If this person is not living, the property shall be distributed according to the terms of my residual clause."

You can direct your executor to divide the residual of your property to one or more persons. If you include very few specific devises in your will, most of your property will pass according to the instructions contained in the residual clause.

Testamentary Trusts

You have the option of creating a complete trust in the residual clause of your will. Your residual clause will then read, "I leave the rest and remainder of my property to John Doe, Trustee. John Doe shall administer the trust as follows." The trust you create inside of your will is called a *testamentary trust*.

The testamentary trust is identical in every single way to a revocable trust that you might have created while you were living, with two very important distinctions. First, the trust is not created until after you are gone. The trust becomes alive after you are dead and is funded and created by the residual clause of your will. Second, the trust document will not include provisions about how to administer the trust property while you are living, because the trust won't be created until after you are gone.

Advantages and Disadvantages

You might create a testamentary trust in your will because you don't want to go through the trouble of transferring all of your property into your name as trustee while you are living as you have to do when creating a revocable trust. But you still want the benefits of creating a trust plan for your family that will govern after you are gone.

It is very important for you to understand that if you create a testamentary trust, your property must be probated. Once the testamentary trust is created in your will, it will be governed by the same rules as a revocable trust, except a testamentary trust remains under the annual supervision of the probate court, because that is where the trust was created.

FACT

A revocable trust you create while you are alive only comes under the supervision of the probate court if someone files a complaint with the probate court about how the trust is being operated.

Taxes

Your will instructs your executor to pay all taxes that are owing—local, state, and federal taxes. The most common taxes owing when a person dies are income taxes or estate and gift taxes. Chapter 18 covers how to compute your federal gift and death tax exposure. (This book does not cover state gift or death taxes, as each state has different rules governing these taxes.)

Your executor will be responsible for filing your final federal and state income tax returns. Most of the rules about how to compute the final income tax returns are the same whether you are living or it is your final return.

If your estate is required to file a federal death tax return, there are elections to take certain deductions on the federal death tax return versus your final income tax return. You should ask the accountant or lawyer who prepares the federal death tax return about these elections.

If you choose to use a will as your planning document, the probate court will not allow your executor to close your estate until he or she has verified that all tax returns have been filed. In most cases, this means that your estate cannot be closed until after January 31 following the year of your death. This is because payers are not required to send the forms and statements that you need to compute the return until January 31. Also, the federal death tax return, if one needs to be filed, is due no later than nine months after the date of your death. Preparing this return may delay the closing of your estate.

The Powers of Your Executor

Your will names the executor, who will be in charge of administering your estate. In some states, the executor is called a personal representative. Your executor is legally responsible for doing everything necessary to probate your estate. (Chapter 7 covers who should serve as your executor, the duties of the executor, and considerations in choosing an executor.) The only document that allows you to appoint an executor is your will.

Your will also defines the powers of your executor. You typically want to give your executor all of the powers to deal with your property that you would have had if you were still alive. You can't anticipate how long it will take to probate your estate. It is difficult to complete the probate process more quickly than six months, and because your executor can't close the estate until all claims have been resolved and all tax returns have been filed, it is quite common for an estate to be open for at least one year. If you restrict the powers your executor has to buy, sell, mortgage, loan, or deal with the estate property, it may hurt your heirs. For example, if you placed a restriction on the executor that he or she cannot sell your property, and your estate holds a particular stock, if the value of the stock begins to decline, your executor will not be able to sell the stock.

If there are certain assets or property you definitely don't want sold or encumbered, you can place a limited restriction on your executor as it relates to that piece of property.

How to Sign

Almost all states require that you sign your will in your own handwriting in the presence of two witnesses and a notary. Some states require that the witnesses be over the age of majority.

Physical Presence Is Mandatory

Although signing your name seems easy enough, there are a couple of things that could create problems. As you know, you must sign in the presence of two witnesses. This can be tricky. You should make sure that you sign the document in the physical presence of the two witnesses who sign in your presence and in the presence of each other. In some states, a will can be found invalid if it is established that the witnesses signed in your presence, but signed at different times. For example, let's say you sign your will in the presence of Witness Number One. And then two hours later, Witness Number Two stops by to sign his name. Because these witnesses did not witness your will in the presence of each other, the will may be invalidated. If you sign your will in the presence of two witnesses, and then the witnesses go to the room next door and sign your will, the witnesses did not sign in your presence, and again, the will might be invalidated.

It's All in the Signature

It is best that you sign your legal name. If the way you normally sign documents is different from your legal name, the probate court judge will usually require testimony from someone who can prove that the way you signed your will is the way you normally sign legal documents. There have been cases where a person signed his will with an *X,* and the will was valid because the person always signed his name with an *X.* It is not the time to be tricky or unusual when you are signing your will. Again, it is highly recommended that you sign your legal name.

Chapter 7

Decisions to Include Within the Will

The more decisions you make for your loved ones while you are living, the easier it will be for them when you are gone. There are several issues that need to be addressed and several choices to be made. However, once you have made it through the decision-making process, drafting the will is not difficult.

Who Will Serve as Your Executor?

The first decision you need to make is who will serve as your executor. Your executor is the person or entity that is in charge of probating your estate after you are gone. You should make this decision in the same way you might decide whether or not you want to become chairperson of a committee. For instance, if you were asked to be chairperson of your homeowner's association, you would probably ask things like, "What do I have to do?" "How much time do you think it will take?" "Will I have help from the neighbors?" "Do you think I'm the best qualified person to serve?" Interestingly enough, these are the same kinds of questions you need to ask regarding who should serve as your executor. When you learn the duties of the executor, you will be prepared to choose the right person or entity to serve.

Your executor needs to be a person or an entity that you trust to handle the job. The duties of your executor will depend on several factors:

- The instructions you put in your will
- The nature and extent of your property
- The special needs of your loved ones
- The possibility that someone will contest your will

Pretend you are writing a job description. The more detailed and specific you are about what you want the executor to do, the easier it will be for him or her to do the job. There are certain duties all executors must perform:

- Locate your will
- Probate your estate
- Decide how and when your property will be distributed

Locating Your Will

The first job for your executor is to locate your original will. You can make this job very easy by simply telling her or him where to find it. However, this requires a great deal of trust. If you are worried that your executor might try to change your will without your permission, you obviously don't want her or him to have access to the original document. You can protect against this possibility by filing your original will with your local probate court for safekeeping. After you are gone, your loved ones can present the probate court with proof of your death, and the original document will already be on file with the court. Or, the lawyer who drafts your will can keep the original will for safekeeping. The important thing is that the executor knows where to find it.

You can also put your original will in a safe-deposit box. If you do this, your executor either needs to have access to the safe-deposit box or be able to contact the person who does have access after you are gone.

Probate Your Estate—Hiring a Lawyer

The executor's next job is to probate your estate. It is almost impossible to probate an estate without the assistance of a lawyer. Many executors think they have to hire the lawyer who drafted the will, no matter how much the lawyer charges. This is not true. Your executor is free to ask the lawyer to hand over the original will, and then shop around and hire a lawyer who will do the best job for the best price. How much lawyers charge to probate an estate varies a great deal. Some charge a percentage of the value of the estate assets, and others charge an hourly fee or a flat fee.

If you think the lawyer is charging too much to prepare your will or will charge too much to probate your estate when you are gone, don't be afraid to shop elsewhere!

It is important for your executor to know how the lawyer bills, and how much the lawyer estimates the job will cost. Here is another opportunity for you to lighten the burden. Ask the lawyer you are thinking about hiring to draft your will not only how much he or she will charge to draft the will, but also how much it will cost to probate your estate after you are gone. Then simply report your findings to the executor.

How and When Your Property Will Be Distributed

The lawyer will prepare the necessary paperwork for the court to probate your estate. Your executor is the one who is left with the job of deciding how and when to distribute your property, unless of course you make those decisions and include the instructions in your will.

The number of decisions your executor needs to make will vary, depending on how specific you were when you created your will. The executor has no choice but to follow the instructions you left. If you give the executor very general instructions, such as "Divide all of my property equally among my children," then the executor is left with the responsibility to decide exactly what each child receives. On the other hand, if you are very specific in your will—for example, "My son should receive my fifty shares of XYZ stock, and my daughter shall receive my ABC mutual fund"—then the executor must distribute the XYZ stock to your son and the ABC mutual fund to your daughter. You have made the decisions about what each child should receive, rather than shifting the responsibility to your executor.

Considerations in Choosing an Executor

Choosing who should serve as executor is very dependent on how specific your will is. If you make most of the decisions while you are living and your will is very specific about what each person is to receive, then it is less important who you name as executor. But if your will is very general, then the job of the executor is much more difficult, and the person you choose to serve must make all of the decisions about what property each person named in your will is to receive. It is much more likely that your loved ones will disagree and perhaps contest the decisions of your executor when you are less specific.

More than one person can serve as your executor. When you name two people to act as executors, both executors must agree on all decisions and sign all of the paperwork. Naming multiple executors to provide a check and balance on the decision-making process makes sense. However, when you name more than two coexecutors, making decisions and executing the necessary paperwork often becomes difficult.

You can also name a professional executor. Banks and trust companies are available to serve as an executor of your will. The fee professional executors charge varies, but it is typically a minimum of $1,500 plus a percentage of the value of your property. Most people who choose a will as their estate-planning document do not name a professional executor.

If any of your loved ones have special needs, this may affect your choice of an executor. For instance, you may choose one child to serve as your executor because you know that child will make the best decisions for the child who has special needs.

Who Should Receive Your Property?

A typical response to this question would be, "I want my spouse to have all of my property when I die, and if my spouse is gone, I want my property divided equally among my children." There are several reasons why this may not be the best plan:

- If your estate is subject to federal death taxes, you probably don't want to leave all of your property outright to your spouse. (Federal death taxes and how to reduce those taxes are covered in Chapters 18 and 19.)
- If this is a second marriage, you may not want to leave all of your property to your spouse.
- If one of your children is not living, you need to decide whether her share will go to her siblings or to her children.
- After a child receives your property, if your child is divorced, you may be concerned about your property going to your child's spouse in a divorce proceeding.

If this is a second marriage, you may want to make sure your spouse has enough income and property for life, but when your spouse is gone you might want your children from a former marriage to receive your property. If this is your objective, a will is not the best estate-planning document for you.

If you want to protect against the possibility that your child will divorce after you are gone and that your child's spouse will take your child's inheritance, you should consider using a trust as your estate-planning document and not a will.

Who you leave your property to is obviously your decision. Take some time and view it from all angles. You need to be assured that your goals will be met and your wishes granted. The best way to do this is to be very specific.

ALERT!

You also need to decide how your property will be distributed if the person to whom you leave the property is not living.

How Should Your Property Be Distributed?

There are three ways you can distribute property in your will:

1. You can draft a will that leaves specific pieces of property to each person.
2. You can draft a will that provides for a fractional division of your property.
3. You can draft a will that has a mix of specific instructions and a fractional division of the remainder of your property.

There are advantages and disadvantages to each method.

Specific Instructions

When you want to leave specific property to named individuals, you will need to make even more decisions before you draft your will.

However, you will have almost eliminated the possibility that your loved ones will disagree, and you have made the job of the executor much easier.

For example, if your will reads, "I leave my property located at 7711 Clinton Drive to my son" and "I leave my property located at 437 Mountain Drive to my daughter," it doesn't matter if the properties are equal in value when you die; the executor must distribute the Clinton Drive property to your son and the Mountain Drive property to your daughter. Putting instructions in your will directing the executor to distribute specific property to each child eliminates the possibility that the children will contest the choice the executor makes about what property to distribute, because they really have no choice. Your will has told the executor what he or she must do.

ESSENTIAL

If you draft a will that distributes specifically described property to each person, you need to review your plan whenever you dispose of property described in the will and determine whether you want to readjust the property to be received by each person.

If your intentions are to treat your children equally, you will have to go through your inventory of property carefully, determine the value of each piece of property, subtract the debt owing against each piece of property, and equalize the end result by deciding which pieces of property to distribute to each child. You may think these are difficult decisions, but if you don't decide what each child is to receive while you are living, the executor must do so after you are gone.

The danger with specific instructions is that if the property is gone, other property cannot be substituted for the property that no longer exists. For example, if your will leaves the property located at 7711 Clinton Drive to your son, and you sell the property before you die and buy a different piece of property with the proceeds, your son will not receive the newly acquired property unless it is specified.

General Instructions

General instructions in a will are much more common than specific instructions. You use general instructions when you want to identify who will receive your property and instruct the executor to make a fractional division of your property. For example, your will might read, "I leave 50 percent of my property to be divided equally between my children and 50 percent to be divided equally among my grandchildren." You have given the executor clear instructions on who should receive your property, but you have provided no guidance on what property each person will receive.

FACT

General instructions in your will on how to distribute your property provide your executor with the least amount of guidance and require him or her to make the decisions you could have made while you are living.

If your executor has been given general instructions on how to distribute your property, and if the persons you name to receive your property cannot agree on what they should receive, any one of the persons can petition the probate court and present arguments about why he or she thinks the proposed distribution is not fair. It is very expensive when your heirs argue over what they are going to receive from your estate. Ultimately the probate court judge might order your executor to sell your property and distribute the cash proceeds rather than the property itself.

A Combination of Instructions

It is much more typical to use a mix of instructions in your will. For example:

I leave my diamond wedding ring to my daughter.
I leave my watch to my son.
I leave my car to my son.

I leave my boat to my daughter.
I direct that the rest of my property be divided equally between
my two children.

The executor must distribute the ring, the watch, the car, and the boat as instructed. These are specific instructions. The executor is then left with the difficult task of deciding how to divide and distribute the rest of your property.

Do You Want Your Property Sold?

Once you analyze each piece of property you own, evaluate the cost of maintaining that property, and consider whether it would be practical for your family to own the property jointly after you are gone. You may be surprised to find you would like to instruct the executor to sell that particular piece of property. The proceeds will then be distributed as you instruct.

If your loved ones disagree and someone petitions the probate court to decide how your property should be divided and distributed, the probate court judge will probably order the executor to sell your property and distribute the cash proceeds.

Your executor has a duty to make prudent financial choices about your property during the course of administering your estate. Your executor may decide that it will cost too much money to maintain the property during the estate administration, and the property should be sold. Or your executor may feel that the property might go down in value and, therefore, decide it is best to sell the property and distribute the cash proceeds.

Of course, if you don't want a particular property sold, you can also stipulate this in your will. Sometimes it is difficult to decide between sentiment and practicality. However, if you don't make these tough decisions yourself, someone else will.

What Is Best for Your Minor Child?

It is very important if you have a minor child to have a will. Your will is the only document that allows you to name a legal guardian for your minor child if you die. If you don't have a will that names a legal guardian, and there is no surviving parent, the probate court will need to conduct a hearing and take testimony from persons interested in serving as legal guardian of the child. When this happens, a person you wouldn't have wanted to raise your child may be appointed the position by the probate court.

The Surviving Parent

If a minor child has a surviving parent, the surviving parent becomes the legal guardian of the child as a matter of law. If you name someone other than the surviving parent as guardian in your will, the attempted appointment will be disregarded. This doesn't prevent an interested person from petitioning the probate court to have the surviving natural parent declared unfit, but this is a separate proceeding that has nothing to do with your will.

Contesting Your Choice

Anyone can contest your choice of legal guardian. The duty of the probate court is to determine what is in the best interest of the minor child. When the will is admitted to probate, various hearings might be scheduled. When there is no surviving parent, the probate court will provide your family with a notice of a hearing to determine the legal guardianship of your minor child. If no one objects at the hearing, the person you name in your will is appointed. But if someone objects, he will bring witnesses and any documentation he has to prove to the court that the person you named as legal guardian is not in the best interest of the minor child.

When you have a will that names a guardian for your minor child, it is very unlikely that a different guardian will be appointed. On the other hand, if you did not make a will to name a legal guardian, the probate court judge must listen to all of the evidence and make an independent determination as to what is in the best interest of your child.

Parents typically have strong preferences about who should raise their children if something happens to them. But the only way to make sure the right person serves, is to create a will naming a guardian.

ALERT!

There is a very strong presumption that the person you name in your will is the person who should be appointed. But the court's primary duty is to ensure the safety of the minor child. If the person contesting proves that the person you name is not fit, a different guardian will be appointed.

How Do You Choose a Guardian?

The answer to this question depends on your family values. You may choose a legal guardian who is most financially able to support the child. Or you may feel it is more important to name a person who will provide for your child's emotional support. Typically, the preferred legal guardian is one whose goals, philosophies, and child-rearing values are most similar to those of the natural parents. Ideally, you should discuss these issues with the person you are considering naming.

There is no legal obligation for you to discuss your choice of guardian or get the approval of the person you have named in your will. However, after you are gone, the legal guardian named must agree to serve. If the person you name is not willing to accept the appointment, the probate court will seek applications from those who do want to serve as legal guardian. Then the probate court will conduct a hearing to make an independent determination about who should be appointed.

ESSENTIAL

Sometimes one or more family members expect to be named as legal guardian of your minor child. If you think a family member would be tremendously hurt if he or she thought you would choose someone else, you might want to avoid discussing this sensitive topic.

The Child's Property

Unless you create a different legal arrangement, the person who is appointed legal guardian of your minor child will also control your child's property. This means that if your will leaves property to your children, the legal guardian will have control over the funds and property. The legal guardian is supposed to use the property for the benefit of your child, but it is very difficult for a minor child to protect his or her property.

When you evaluate all of the property your child would receive from you if you and your spouse died, you may decide that you don't want the guardian to have control of it. If this is your decision, you need to create a trust for your child's property, and name someone to serve as trustee.

It is possible to create a trust for your minor child in your will, called a testamentary trust. It would contain specific instructions about who should serve as trustee for the benefit of the property of your minor child. The trust would also contain instructions on how your property should be managed and distributed. This trust would come into existence only when you died. If you want to create a trust for your child's property, you should read Chapters 11 through 14. (E)

Chapter 8
Drafting Your Will

You have multiple options about how to draft your will. You can buy forms from your local office supply store, download forms from the Internet, or purchase inexpensive software packages that will create a will for you. Of course, you can also hire a lawyer to prepare the document.

Filling in a Form Will

Some office supply stores still carry paper will forms you can buy. These forms allow you to fill in the blanks to create your will. However, it is difficult for such a form to meet everyone's needs. A will that might meet the goals and objectives for one family will often be different from a will that meets the needs of another family, even when the two families seem similar. Frankly, it is hard to even find an office supply store that still sells paper forms. Most now sell computer software packages instead that will generate wills, as well as other common estate-planning documents.

You may not be comfortable with computers and prefer the old-fashioned method. If you can't locate a paper form, you can use the information you learned in Chapters 6 and 7 and the sample will found in this chapter to help you draft your own will.

ALERT!

You need to be careful when you use any self-help methods of creating a will. The words in a will have very specific meanings, and can have surprising results if you don't understand the definitions and the rules.

Internet Forms

There are hundreds of Web sites where you can find a form will. Some of the Web sites allow you to download the document free of charge, while others charge a fee for the download. Some documents are in PDF format and cannot be changed, and others are downloaded into a word processing format. There are also Web sites that have interactive forms, allowing you to create a will online and download the finished document. Most of the interactive Web sites charge a fee.

The problem with obtaining information on the Internet is that you have no way of judging the accuracy or reliability of the information or forms you find. However, the American Bar Association has recommended that the state bar associations begin providing self-help legal information on the state bar association Web sites. The sentiment seems to be that if a state bar association is providing information on the

Internet, it will be accurate and reliable. Visit ✑ *www.bestcase.com/ statebar.htm* to find the bar association in your state.

Books

There are books that contain legal forms, but it is difficult to find a book that is devoted exclusively to will forms. There are publications that teach you about estate planning, but these books tend to cover some topics in such complicated terms that it is difficult to get what is often referred to as "meat and potatoes advice."

If you reviewed every book that is used in the law schools to teach law students about wills, you would find that these publications begin with the history of the statute of wills enacted in England in the 1500s and address every possible facet of will law, probate, and litigation to contest a will.

If you have the time to read a 1,000-plus-page textbook on wills, it can be fascinating. But most people simply want to understand the parts of a will and the terminology they need to understand to make the right choices for their family. Of course, they also want guidance and forms to get the job done. Unfortunately, books specific to wills that include the legal forms you need are not easy to come by.

ESSENTIAL

The rules you must follow to create a valid will can vary slightly from state to state. If you draft your own will, even with the best form available, it's a good idea to have your document checked by a lawyer who is licensed in your state. This will assure that your will is valid and that it has been signed following the proper formalities.

Handwritten Wills

You need to be very careful with handwritten wills. A handwritten will is really a slang term. A handwritten will typically refers to a will that you write in your own handwriting and did not sign in the presence of two witnesses and a notary.

If you write out your will, date the document, and sign your name in the presence of two witnesses and a notary, you have a perfectly valid will. However, it isn't a good idea to write your will in your own handwriting, even if you sign the document in the presence of two witnesses and a notary. You are more likely to make a mistake or use words that may be confusing to the probate court.

Using Computer Software

There are numerous computer software programs that allow you to create your own will. Some of the programs have wills you can print and then you fill in the blanks. Most of the programs guide you though a questionnaire regarding who you would like to serve as your executor and how you would like your property distributed. When you complete the questionnaire, the computer program generates a will for you.

Computer-software-generated wills can be very good. The programs ask you very straightforward questions, then take your answers and convert your instructions into a will. When you use any computer program to create your will, it is very important that you understand the questions the program is asking. The computer program cannot read your mind. It can only generate a will in response to your answers.

Hiring a Lawyer to Prepare the Will

A lawyer understands the legal significance of the technical words and can make sure you sign your will with the proper formalities. A lawyer can also advise you about any unusual laws that might exist in your state about inheriting property and advise you regarding any exposure your estate might have to federal or state death taxes.

If you hire a lawyer to prepare your will, most of the lawyer's time will be spent teaching you the same rules you will learn in this book and learning about your family and your property. If you are prepared, you will save a great deal of money when you hire a lawyer.

Sample Will

When a lawyer completes your will, it will look similar to the sample will contained in this section. The information specific to the hypothetical client, Jane, is in bold.

LAST WILL AND TESTAMENT
OF
JANE A. DOE

I, **JANE A. DOE**, a resident of **Sarasota County, Florida**, do make, publish, and declare this to be my Last Will and Testament, hereby revoking all former wills and codicils.

I.
DECLARATIONS

My husband is **JOHN ALEXANDER DOE**. I have **two (2) children, JACK JOSEPH DOE and JAMIE ANN DOE.** Except as otherwise qualified, the words "child" or "children" when used in this Will with reference to me shall mean all my above-named children. The words "child" or "children" when used in this Will with reference to any person other than me **shall mean all natural and adopted children** including natural children born after the death of their parent **but excluding stepchildren and foster children.** The word "descendants" when used in this Will shall mean all of the person's lineal descendants of all generations, except those who are descendants of a living descendant, with the relationship of parent and child at each generation being determined under governing law. To be a child or descendant by virtue of adoption, the person must be adopted while a minor.

II.
PAYMENT OF DEBTS

I direct payment of all debts enforceable against me during my lifetime which are presented in a timely manner during the administration of my estate, the expenses of my last illness and funeral, burial, cemetery marker, cremation, or other disposition of my body, and the expenses of administration of my estate, provided that if any property (including life insurance) owned by me jointly, or individually, passing under this Will or otherwise, shall be encumbered by a mortgage, pledge, security interest, loan, lien, or unpaid taxes, the indebtedness secured by such encumbrance shall not be charged to or paid by my estate but such property shall pass subject to all encumbrances existing at my death.

III.

<u>SPECIFIC DEVISES OF TANGIBLE PERSONAL PROPERTY</u>

(1) I devise **to my husband**, if he survives me, all my clothing, jewelry, watches, household goods, personal effects, motor vehicles, household furniture and fixtures, dishes, china, silver, athletic and sporting equipment, books, collections, yard and maintenance equipment, tools, works of art, antiques, and all other tangible personal property (excluding therefrom tangible personal property owned by me and used in connection with any business I may own) not heretofore specifically devised or otherwise effectually disposed of, such items hereinafter referred to collectively as my "personal property." Further, I may leave a list or other document directing certain items of my personal property to particular children or other persons. If I do this, I request that my bequests be honored.

(2) If **my husband** fails to survive me, I devise my personal property and the tangible personal property of a similar nature received by me from **my husband** at his death, **to my surviving children** (or all to one if only one survives), **to be divided by them as they agree, or if they fail to agree within six (6) months after my death, in equal shares, the assets constituting such equal shares to be determined by my Executor, whose decision shall be final and binding on all interested parties.**

(3) **If my husband and children all fail to survive me,** these specific devises shall lapse and become part of the residue of my estate.

(4) All expenses incurred in the safeguarding and delivery of tangible personal property, including, without limitation, storage, packing, shipping, and insurance expenses, shall be treated as an expense of the administration of my estate and shall not be charged against the devisee who receives such tangible personal property.

(5) I devise all of my insurance policies that provide indemnity for the loss of any of my personal or real property by fire, windstorm, or other similar casualty (including any claim for the loss of any such property that I might have at the time of my death against any insurance company) to those persons or entities who shall become the owners of such properties by reason of my death, whether such ownership be acquired under the provisions of this Will or otherwise.

IV.
RESIDUARY DEVISE

All the rest and residue of my estate, wherever situated, including lapsed devises, but expressly excluding any property over which I may have power of appointment at my death, **I devise to my husband, JOHN ALEXANDER DOE. In the event he predeceases me, my residuary estate shall be distributed to my children, JACK JOSEPH DOE and JAMIE ANN DOE, in equal shares, per stirpes.**

If my husband and all my children and their descendants all fail to survive me, I devise said residue to the SOUTHEASTERN DOG RESCUE, INC., 1234 Puppy Lane, Anytown, FL 12345, (555) 555-5555.

V.
TAXES

All inheritance, estate, succession, transfer, and other death taxes, both federal and state, including any interest or penalties thereon, charged against my estate or any person or entity, which become payable by reason of my death, whether in respect to property passing under this Will or otherwise, except any taxes imposed on any generation-skipping transfer under Chapter 13 of the United States Internal Revenue Code of 1954, as amended, or any corresponding provision of any future United States law, and except taxes attributable to any taxable power of appointment I have, shall be paid out of the residue of my probate estate without apportionment and no part thereof shall be charged back or imposed on any such person or entity. My Executor shall have the power to select tax years and make all other decisions and elections permitted under any applicable income, estate, or inheritance tax law, including the imposition of a lien on estate assets to secure tax payments, without regard to the effect thereof, if any, on any devisee of my estate, and, if any such decision or election shall be made, to apportion, or refrain from apportioning, the consequences thereof among the devisees of my estate, all in such manner as my Executor shall deem appropriate. If my Executor in good faith decides that there is uncertainty as to the inclusion of particular property in my gross estate for federal estate tax purposes, then such property may, in the discretion of my Executor, be excluded from my gross estate in my federal estate tax return. The decision of my Executor as to the date that should be selected for the valuation of property in my gross estate for federal estate tax purposes shall be conclusive on all concerned.

VI.
SURVIVORSHIP

Any devisee of this Will who dies within sixty (60) days after my death shall be deemed to have failed to survive me and this Will shall be interpreted and my estate administered as though I had survived such devisee.

VII.
NO CONTRACT

This Will is being executed on even date with a Will of my husband, but in no event shall said Wills be considered joint and/or mutual. It is my express intent that the survivor of myself and my husband shall in no way be restricted thereby in the use, management, enjoyment, or disposition of our estates or his separate estate by subsequent gift, will, or sale.

VIII.
ADMINISTRATIVE POWERS OF EXECUTOR

I give to my Executor, in addition to and not in limitation of all common law and statutory powers, the following powers: to retain any estate asset at any time received, for such period as my Executor shall deem advisable; to invest or reinvest in any property, real or personal; to sell, exchange, lease, give options upon, partition, or otherwise dispose of any property, real or personal, in my estate, at public or private sale, without regard to the necessity of such sale for the purpose of paying debts, taxes, or legacies, for cash or other consideration or on credit and upon such terms and conditions as my Executor deems advisable; to adjust, compromise, and settle all matters of business and claims in favor of or against my estate; to insure, repair, maintain, and preserve property; to retain and continue any business or business interest in which I am engaged or which I own; to give proxies and hold or register securities in the name of a nominee, a securities depositor, or in any other form convenient for my estate; to exercise any stock option or any other kind of option; to join in mergers, reorganizations, joint creditors actions, or other similar arrangements; to allocate and apportion receipts and disbursements to income or principal reasonably and in accordance with sound estate accounting principles; to sue for tax refunds; to borrow in the name of my estate, including the right to borrow from a corporate Executor or any affiliate, and in connection therewith, to mortgage, pledge, or encumber estate assets, provided my Executor shall not be personally liable and that any such loan shall be payable out of estate assets only; to join in the filing of joint income or gift tax returns with my husband; to petition for the appointment of or actually appoint an ancillary estate fiduciary and to pay the expenses of ancillary administration; to distribute my estate in cash or in kind, or partly in cash and partly in kind, as my Executor deems advisable, and to satisfy a specific dollar amount devise in kind, in the discretion of my Executor, and, for purposes of distribution, to value assets reasonably and in good faith as of the date of distribution, provided that my Executor shall not be required to distribute a proportionate amount of each asset to each devisee but may instead make non pro-rata distributions, and provided further, that in making distributions, my Executor may, but shall not be required to, take account of the income tax basis in relation to market value of assets distributed; to distribute assets directly to the devisee, to a legally appointed Guardian or Conservator or, whereby permitted by law, to a custodian under any Uniform Gifts to Minors Act, including a custodian selected by my Executor; and to do any and all things necessary or proper to complete the administration of my estate, all as fully as I could do if living. All such powers may be exercised without application to any court and shall be exercisable by any alternate, survivor, or successor Executor(s).

IX.
EXECUTOR

I appoint JOHN ALEXANDER DOE as Executor. In the event JOHN ALEXANDER DOE cannot serve, I appoint my daughter, JAMIE ANN DOE, as Executor. If JAMIE ANN DOE cannot serve, I appoint JACK JOSEPH DOE as Executor. I direct that no bond be required of any executor named in this Will.

IN WITNESS WHEREOF, I have set my hand and seal to this, my Last Will and Testament, consisting of this and the preceding **(insert number of pages)** typewritten pages, and the witness provisions hereinafter, and for the purpose of identification I have signed this and the preceding pages, all in the presence of the persons witnessing it at my request at Sarasota County, Florida, on this _____ day of June, 200____.

_____

JANE A. DOE

On this ____ day of June, 200____, **JANE A. DOE** declared to us, the undersigned, that the foregoing instrument consisting of these witness provisions and the foregoing **(insert number of pages)**, was her Last Will and Testament and she requested us to act as witnesses to the same and to her signature thereon. She thereupon signed said Will in our presence, we being present at the same time. We now, at her request, in her presence, and in the presence of each other, do hereunto subscribe our names as witnesses. We, and each of us declare that we believe this Testatrix to be of sound mind and memory.

WITNESSES:

_____

Witness Number One

_____

Witness Number Two

AFFIDAVIT OF EXECUTION

STATE OF FLORIDA
COUNTY OF SARASOTA

We, **JANE A. DOE [Insert Name Witness 1], and [Insert Name Witness 2],** the Testatrix and the witnesses, respectively, whose names are signed to the attached or foregoing instrument, having been sworn, declared to the undersigned officer that the Testatrix, in the presence of witnesses, signed the instrument as the Testatrix's Last Will, that the Testatrix signed, and that each of the witnesses, in the presence of the Testatrix and in the presence of each other, signed the Will as a witness.

_____

JANE A. DOE

WITNESSES:

_____

Witness Number One

_____

Witness Number Two

Subscribed and sworn to before me by **JANE A. DOE**, the Testatrix who is personally known to me or who has produced _____ as identification, and by **[Insert Name Witness 1]**, a witness who is personally known to me or who has produced _____ as identification, and by **[Insert Name Witness 2]**, a witness who is personally known to me or who has produced _____ as identification, on this ____ day of June, 200____.

_____

Signature of Notary Public
Sarasota County, Florida
My Commission Expires:

Don't forget that it is very important that you and the two witnesses are all in the presence of one another when each signs his or her name. If you and the witnesses are not together when you sign, your will can be found invalid after you are gone.

Some states require that your will have an Affidavit of Execution, like the one found in the sample document. The Affidavit must be signed in the presence of the same two witnesses and a notary. It's a good idea to make sure your will would meet the requirement of any state where you might live.

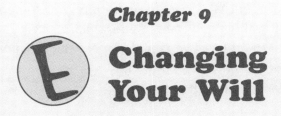

Chapter 9

Changing Your Will

There are very few things in your life that stay the same forever. Your life changes, as do the lives of your loved ones. You need to know how to change your will to accommodate those changing needs. It is not difficult to change your will; you just need to know the rules.

Four Ways to Change Your Will

It is not difficult to change your will, but you need to be sure you follow the proper formalities. If you don't make the changes correctly, you may actually make your entire will invalid. The formalities you need to follow may not make sense to you, but they exist to make sure that someone does not change your will without your permission. Unfortunately, the same rules that are meant to protect you can also make the document you intended to be your will invalid.

There are four ways to change your will:

1. You can make and sign a new document.
2. You can amend your will.
3. You can strike one or more provisions.
4. You can insert changes into the existing document.

Each of these will have formalities that must be followed to make the change valid.

Make a New Document

The best way to change your will is to make a new one. In the old days, making a new will meant typing a new document. Today almost everyone has access to a word processor. Making the changes you want is as easy as pushing the delete button and inserting the changes. When you make a new will, it gives you a chance to review all of the provisions of the old will. By the time you are ready to alter your will, you may own different property, and it's likely that the needs of your loved ones have changed.

Repeating the Process

When you change your will, you should again ask yourself who, what, where, when, and why. Who is receiving your property, what are they receiving, where are they going to take possession of the property, when do you want them to have the property, and why. When you follow this process regarding each piece of property you own, it is much more likely that your instructions will be clear, minimizing the possibility that someone will contest your will. Think of the process as a game—the players and the property are constantly changing.

When you make a new will, make sure that you sign it in the presence of two witnesses and a notary. You need to sign the new will with the same formalities you followed when you signed your original will.

The Former Will

When you revoke your old will by making a new will, you need to be very careful that your new will specifically states that you are making a new will and that it completely revokes all prior wills. The reason you want to be very specific is because if the new will does not say that all old wills are revoked and an old will is found, both documents could be admitted to probate. Then, your property will be distributed according to the provisions of both documents.

For example, assume you sign your first will and leave $50,000 to your friend Jane. Three years later, you sign will number two. You intended will number two to revoke will number one, but it does not specifically state that will number one is revoked. Will number two leaves $100,000 to Jane. If will number two does not revoke will number one, Jane might receive both the $50,000 distribution from will number one and $100,000 from will number two. This may not be what you intended, but you are not alive to tell the probate court what you did intend.

When you make a new will it is highly recommended that you destroy the old will and all copies of the old will. This is not the time to keep your old papers to memorialize what you wanted several years ago. You don't want multiple wills presented to the probate court after you are gone.

Strike a Provision

You can change your will by striking one or more provisions. If a person contests, seeking a distribution of the property, your executor must prove that you struck the provision with the intent to revoke that provision. There needs to be proof because the court wants to be satisfied that you were the person who struck the provision and that the provision was struck with the intent to revoke it.

Family Fights Get Expensive

To show how important proof is, let's say your daughter finds your original will in your desk drawer. She discovers that you left your business to her brother and the rest of your property to her and your son equally. She takes out a pen and strikes the provision leaving the business to her brother. She then puts the will back in the desk drawer.

After you are gone, your daughter argues that you wanted all of your property divided equally between her and her brother. Your son, on the other hand, will need to introduce evidence to the probate court that you did not strike the provision regarding the business, and that he is entitled to the business and the rest of your property should be divided between him and his sister. Your daughter will hire a lawyer to argue her position, your son will need to hire a lawyer to prove that you did not strike the provision, and the executor must hire a lawyer to represent the estate's interest. It gets very expensive when your family fights over what you intended.

Proving Your Intent

If you change your document by striking a provision and someone contests, there will be a hearing before the probate court judge to prove your intent. The lawyer for the estate might try to prove your intent by calling witnesses who were with you and saw you strike the provision. But if the witness has an interest in your property, the probate court judge might not believe her. Or perhaps you signed your name or initialed the document when you struck the provision. If you did not sign or initial the change in the presence of two witnesses and a notary, again the lawyer for the estate must prove that it is your initial or signature and that it is evidence that you intended to make the change. If your will was in a secure place, such as your safe-deposit box, proof may be available that you were the only one with access to the will, and therefore the change had to be made by you. Because of the need to prove your intent, striking a provision is not the best way to change your will.

Make Written Changes

It is very common for a person to try to change his or her will by making written changes to the existing document. Let's say you do one of the following:

- Write on the back of the will, "I hereby revoke this will."
- Write on the last page of the will, "I hereby revoke this will."
- Insert a handwritten change to the will.

If you did not sign your name to the written change in the presence of two witnesses and a notary, the attempt to change or revoke your will is not valid. You could argue that the need to have two witnesses and a notary for a change is unnecessary. But it doesn't matter if the whole world knew that you wanted to make the change or revoke the document. You are not available to tell the probate court what you wanted, and the rules are designed to protect against someone making a change without your permission. Since you need to sign your name to any changes you make to your will in the presence of two witnesses and a notary, you might as well just make a new will!

FACT

In the old days, wills were typed on a typewriter. To avoid retyping the will, people were tempted to just write changes on the existing document. Modern technology makes it so easy to have your will on a computer. Changes can easily be made, and a new will can be printed and then signed by you in the presence of two witnesses and a notary.

Add an Amendment

You can also make a change by adding an amendment to your will. This is called a *codicil* to your will. If you choose to change your will with a codicil, you should:

- Make your changes on a separate piece of paper.
- State that you are changing your will.
- Identify the date of the original will you are changing.
- Write down the changes you want.
- Sign the amendment in the presence of two witnesses and a notary.

When you change your will with a codicil, you need to make sure that the changes you are making are clear and do not create conflicts with any of the provisions in your original will. For example, assume you want to change your executor. Your codicil would look like the example on the facing page.

John Doe and the two witnesses should sign their names to the codicil in the presence of two witnesses and a notary. The notary will then sign the codicil and stamp it with his or her notary stamp.

The more complicated the changes you want to make, the harder it is to change your will with a codicil. If your changes are confusing, you run the risk that a loved one will not understand what you wanted and will contest your will. Because a codicil needs to be signed with the same formalities required to sign a will, it is usually better to make the changes and reprint a whole new will.

Destroy the Document

You can revoke your will by the physical act of burning, tearing, or obliterating it. When you revoke your will by physical act, the executor bears the burden of proving that the physical act was done with the intent to revoke your will. This is not a foolproof way to revoke your will—unless you destroy the original and all copies of your will.

If you only destroy your original will and someone happens to find a

CODICIL TO WILL

I, John Doe, on this 10th day of May, 2003, hereby execute this Codicil to my will dated February 1, 1997. I hereby revoke the portion of Article X that named Bill Smith as my Executor. I hereby name David Jones to serve as Executor.

Witnesses:

_____   _____
Anna Miller   John Doe

_____
Betty White
County of Sarasota
State of Florida

On this 10th day of May, 2003, personally appeared John Doe. John Doe executed a Codicil to his will, originally executed on the 1st day of February, 1997. John Doe executed his Codicil in the presence of the two witnesses, Anna Miller and Betty White. Anna Miller and Betty White are over the age of 21 and believe John Doe is of sound mind.

_____
Notary, Sarasota County, Florida
My commission expires on _____

copy of it, they can try to introduce the copy to the probate court. However, the person introducing the copy has the burden of proving that you did not destroy the document with the intent to revoke. Although this can be difficult for someone to prove, whenever someone contests anything about your will, the person contesting must hire a lawyer to present his or her case, and your executor has to hire a lawyer to represent the estate.

FACT

The reason for having the witnesses sign in your physical presence is to minimize the chance that someone would take your document and make changes without your permission. Remember, the formalities are meant to protect against someone changing your will or codicil without your permission.

Control of the Original Will

Who has control of the original will can affect whether or not a change you made will be valid. Your original is likely in one of the following places:

- In your possession, typically in your home
- In a safe-deposit box
- With your lawyer
- On file with the probate court

In Your Possession

When your original will is in your possession, issues can arise regarding whether any changes were made. The more people who have physical access to your will, the greater the chance an alteration to the will can be made without your permission.

Perhaps you are thinking about making a change. For example, assume you take your will out of your desk, and you make some notes on the document or put a line through several provisions. You aren't certain you are ready to make the change, so you put your will back into the desk drawer. You die. When the document is admitted to probate, there will probably be a debate about whether you struck certain provisions with the intent to revoke them or were merely thinking about making changes. Your intent will become an issue that will be decided by the probate court judge. The probate court does not know what you wanted. You are gone. Your executor will have to look for evidence to prove your intent.

In a Safe-Deposit Box

The significance of having your will in your safe-deposit box depends on who had access to the box while you were alive. If someone has access to your safe-deposit box, he or she could remove your will and make changes without your permission. Even if you were the only one with access, you might bring your will home where someone could alter the document there. The fact that the will was kept in the safe-deposit box may or may not affect how your executor proves whether or not a change was made to your will, but you should be aware of the possibility.

With Your Lawyer

When your lawyer keeps the original will, the chance that changes were made without your permission is minimal. No self-respecting lawyer would allow you to make a change to your document without having you sign a document that makes the changes in the presence of two witnesses and a notary. If you leave your original will with your lawyer, you need to make sure your loved ones know how to contact him or her.

ALERT!

Unless you have interviewed and documented how the lawyer is going to bill to probate your estate when you are gone and a decision has been made, you need to remind your family that they don't have to hire that lawyer to probate your estate merely because he or she has possession of the original will.

On File with the Probate Court

If you put your original will on deposit with the probate court in the county where you are living, you are the only person who has access to the will. When you want to make changes, you can do so and then return the new changed will to the probate court. Having the document on deposit with the probate court minimizes the chance that someone other than you will alter your will. If you remove your will from the probate court to make changes, you need to be sure to make the desired changes with the necessary formalities.

It is not difficult to change your will, but it is important that you make the changes correctly. Otherwise, the probate court will invalidate your will or a portion of your will, and your intentions will be defeated. The best way to change your will is to make a new one.

A Lawyer Isn't Necessary

When you understand the rules about how to change your will, you do not need a lawyer. You just need to be careful that you are making the changes correctly and that the formalities to make the changes valid have been met. Even if you follow the rules, it is possible that someone will challenge your will and allege that you were not the one who made the change. Remember, when you are gone, you are not available to tell the probate court what you wanted.

While not necessary, sometimes enlisting the help of a lawyer is in your best interests. If you have your lawyer change your will, he or she will talk to you about your changes and have you sign your will or codicil in the presence of two witnesses and a notary. The lawyer and his or her staff will be available to testify, if needed. This assures that the changes you want will be found valid after you are gone. Ⓔ

Chapter 10

Owning Property in Joint Name

Owning property in joint name is the simplest way for you to leave property to your loved ones. But it is important to understand that simple is not always the best. There are advantages and disadvantages you should consider before you decide that joint ownership is the estate plan for you.

The Joint-Property Estate Plan

How many times have you heard the statement, "I don't need an estate plan, we own all of our property in joint name"? Joint property is a simple estate plan, but you need to weigh the advantages and disadvantages. As long as all of the joint tenants do not die in a common accident, joint property will pass automatically to the surviving joint tenant(s) when you die, avoiding probate.

For some people, owning property in joint name is their entire plan. For others, owning property in joint name is part of the estate plan. Get out those sheets of paper that describe each piece of property you own, and prepare to calculate the consequences of owning property in joint name. When you know the rules, you will be able to decide whether joint property is the best plan for you.

Advantages and Disadvantages

The primary advantage of owning property in joint name with another person is that when you are gone, your property passes automatically to the surviving joint tenant. If you own property with one joint tenant, the surviving joint tenant will own 100 percent of the property after you are gone. If you own property with more than one joint tenant, the property will pass in equal shares to the surviving joint tenants.

Unexpected Consequences

Owning property in joint name is a simple way to have title to your property pass when you are gone, but there can be unexpected consequences when you create the joint tenancy and when you die. There are several reasons that you may not want to place all of your property in joint name with another person or persons.

When you place most types of property in joint name with another person, you have made an irrevocable decision. If you change your mind about owning your property with the person you added as a joint tenant, you can't get the property back without the permission of your new joint tenant. Also, with most types of property, when you add a person as a joint tenant, you have made a taxable gift to that person. You will need to read Chapter 18 to learn the rules about gift taxes.

Bank Accounts

There is an exception to the rule that you make an irrevocable decision and a taxable gift when you add a person as a joint tenant to your bank accounts. When you add a person's name to your bank account, you are usually creating a joint tenancy. You need to ask your financial institution to outline the rights created when you add a name to your bank account. The rights created can vary among financial institutions. You have not made an irrevocable decision because you are not treated as having made a gift until the person whose name you added withdraws money that he or she did not deposit.

ALERT!

Beware! Any joint tenant can withdraw all of the funds from the account. Even though the decision to add a person's name to your bank account is not irrevocable, you might wake up one morning and find all of your money gone.

Your Will Doesn't Affect Joint Property

This is probably one of the most misunderstood concepts. Your will has absolutely no effect on joint property. As a matter of fact, your will could say, "I leave the funds in XYZ Bank in equal shares to my children," but such a clause would be ignored if the bank account is in joint name. If you have four children but you have put one child's name on your bank account, the entire balance will belong to the child named on the account, and will not pass in equal shares to all of your children. Remember, one reason you put your property in joint name was so that title would pass automatically to the joint tenant when you die.

Imagine the shock and disappointment of your children who are not joint tenants on your property. The other children will wonder whether you loved the child you included as a joint tenant more than them. You may have put one child's name on an account as a matter of convenience. But after you are gone, your children have no way of knowing what you really intended.

Jointly Owned Property with Your Spouse

Joint ownership of property between spouses makes a lot of sense. But like most things, you need to consider whether any of the disadvantages of owning property in joint name with your spouse apply to you. The main advantage to owning property in joint name with your spouse is simplicity. When the first spouse dies, the surviving spouse owns the property and doesn't need to probate the property to obtain title.

There are three potential disadvantages to owning property in joint name with your spouse. First, your surviving spouse loses an income tax advantage he or she might have had if the property had not been owned in joint name. Second, if the property owned by both spouses is subject to federal death taxes, it can cost a family a considerable amount of money. Third, joint ownership does not allow the spouse who died first to have any control over what the surviving spouse does with the property.

ESSENTIAL

There are differences among states about how property passes when a joint tenant dies. Most problems that arise after a person dies relate to confusion about how the property was actually titled. You should confirm with a lawyer in your state exactly how your property should be titled in order for it to be treated as joint property with survivorship rights.

Income Tax Consequences

There are special income tax rules that apply to property owned as joint tenants by spouses. To understand the potential disadvantage, you need to learn the rules about cost basis. When you die, all of the property you own on the date of your death will get a new cost basis equal to the fair market value of the property at that time. Cost basis is the amount you subtract from the sale price of the property to compute your gain or loss when you sell a piece of property.

For example, assume you bought one share of ABC stock for $10; $10 is your cost basis. Now assume you die when the stock is worth $90 a share. You owned the stock in your individual name and not in joint tenancy with your spouse, and you leave the stock to your spouse in your will. Your spouse will get a new cost basis in the stock equal to $90. If your spouse sells the stock later for $95, your spouse's gain on the sale will be $5 ($95 sale price minus $90 cost basis). If you had sold the stock while you were alive for $95, you would have had an $85 gain ($95 sale price minus your cost basis of $10).

FACT

If you believe one spouse is likely to pass away first, you should consider placing the property in the individual name of the spouse that is likely to die, rather than in joint name. The surviving spouse will then receive a full increase in cost basis, if one year passes after the transfer of the property.

However, the rules are different if you own property in joint name with your spouse. As you know, when you own property in joint name with your spouse, the spouse owns the property automatically. But your surviving spouse only receives a 50 percent increase in cost basis plus half of his or her original basis. Let us return to the same example. You paid $10 for the one share of stock in ABC Company and put the stock in joint name with your spouse. You die when the stock is worth $90. Your spouse has a cost basis of 50 percent of the fair market value of the stock when you died, or $45, plus he gets to add half of what you paid for the stock, or $5. Your surviving spouse's cost basis is $45 plus $5. Now when he sells the share of ABC Company stock for $95, he has a $45 gain ($95 sale price minus $50 cost basis). Compare this to the $5 gain he would have had if you had left the share to your spouse in your will. This is a very important consequence to owning property in joint name with your spouse, since the gain may be subject to income taxes.

IRS Rules

Are there any hidden tricks? Yes. The IRS rules require one year to pass between the time you transfer property back to your surviving spouse. For example, assume you paid $10 for the one share of ABC Company stock. You placed the stock in joint name with your spouse and then received some bad medical news. If you transfer the share of ABC Company stock back into your individual name and then leave the stock to your spouse in your will, you must live one year after you transferred the share back into your name before you die. If this one year passes and the stock is worth $90 when you die, your spouse will get a new cost basis equal to $90. But if you do not live that one year, your spouse will take the same cost basis he or she would have had in the joint tenancy. In this example, the property was owned in joint name and would have resulted in a new cost basis of $50 had the spouse received the stock as the surviving joint tenant.

FACT

When spouses own property in joint name, they sacrifice an increase in cost basis for the simplicity associated with the fact that joint property passes automatically to the surviving joint spouse.

Property May Go Down in Value

The surviving spouse gets a new cost basis equal to the value of the property you own when you die. If your property has gone down in value, and you leave the property to your surviving spouse, she will take the lower value as her cost basis. For example, assume you bought one share of DEF stock for $100. The stock is worth $20 when you die. If the stock was in joint name with your spouse, her new cost basis would be $60—half of what you paid ($50), plus half of the value of the stock when you died, or $10 ($50 + $10 = $60). If the stock of DEF had been in your individual name, your spouse would have a cost basis equal to the value of the stock on the date of your death, $20.

In this case, joint ownership with your spouse gives you a better cost basis. You would like the cost basis to be as high as possible. If your spouse sells the one share of DEF stock that had been owned in joint name for $20, she will have a loss on her return of $40 (sale price of $20 minus cost basis of $60 equals $40 loss). If you had owned the stock in your individual name and left the stock to your spouse, she would not have any gain or loss if she sold the stock for $20 (sale price of $20 minus cost basis of $20 equals no gain or loss).

ALERT!

If you think the income tax cost basis rules could be a disadvantage, you need to read Chapter 18 about federal death taxes. In certain circumstances, owning all of your property in joint name with your spouse could cost your family $345,500 in unnecessary federal death taxes. Chapter 19 teaches you how this result could be avoided.

When you summarize information about each piece of property you own on a separate piece of paper for your notebook, you should compute the cost basis for each. Calculate the cost basis your spouse would receive if you owned your property in joint name and compare it with the cost basis he or she would receive if your property was owned in your individual name. This may help you plan.

Loss of Control

When you own all of your property in joint name with your spouse, you have no control over what your spouse does with your property when you are gone. Many people say this doesn't matter, because they are confident that their spouse is capable of managing the property. But the world is a more complicated place than it was in days gone by.

There are ways you can leave property to your spouse and not have to worry about whether your spouse will be sued and lose the property, or whether someone will try to take advantage of him or her when you are gone. Before you make the decision to own your property in joint name, you should read Chapters 11 through 14 and consider the advantages of creating a trust for your spouse.

FACT

You need to analyze the cost basis of the property that will be acquired by your surviving joint tenants. The cost basis rules are different for spouses who are joint tenants, and all other joint tenants. You should also calculate the federal death tax exposure that may be created for your surviving joint tenants.

Joint Property with Someone Else

The basic rule that the property passes automatically to the surviving joint tenant is the same whether your joint tenant is your spouse or someone else. However, the income tax cost basis rules are different. For persons who are not your spouse, the surviving joint tenant gets an increase in cost basis equal to the percentage of contribution to the acquisition cost of the property made by the person who just died.

For example, assume you and your brother purchase a piece of property and put the title in your joint names. Assume the property cost $100,000. You contributed $40,000, which equals 40 percent of the purchase price. Your brother contributed $60,000 to the purchase price. You die when the property is worth $200,000. Your brother keeps his original cost basis of $60,000, the amount he paid for the property, plus he will increase his cost basis by $80,000. The increase in your brother's cost basis is the percentage of the purchase price you contributed, 40 percent, times the value of the property when you die (40% × $200,000 = $80,000). Your brother's new cost basis is $60,000 + $80,000 = $140,000. If your brother sells the property for $210,000 after you are gone, your brother will have a $70,000 gain ($210,000 selling price minus his cost basis of $140,000).

This rule can work very nicely when parents place property in joint name with their children and pay for the entire purchase price. For example, assume you place the same property worth $100,000 in joint name with your daughter. You pay the entire purchase price of $100,000.

You die when the property is worth $200,000. Your daughter will rece the property automatically because she is the surviving joint tenant. Because your daughter contributed nothing toward the purchase price of the property, she gets a 100 percent increase in cost basis. This is because the surviving joint tenant who is not a spouse increases his or her basis equal to the percentage the person who died contributed to the purchase of the property. You contributed 100 percent, therefore your daughter gets 100 percent of the value of the property at the date of your death as her new cost basis. Therefore, if the property is worth $200,000 when you die, her new cost basis is $200,000. But remember, when you placed the property in joint name with your daughter, you made an irrevocable gift of 50 percent of the property. Chapter 18 teaches you the rules about gift taxes.

QUESTION?

Is it a good plan to place property in joint name with your children?
It can be. The child will receive the property automatically as the surviving joint tenant. The child also gets a full increase in cost basis (assuming the child contributed nothing to the acquisition). But the parent cannot change his or her mind. The gift is irrevocable, unless it is a bank account.

Multiple Joint Tenants

You can have as many joint tenants as you want. Assume your spouse is gone, and you have two children. You decide to add the children as joint tenants on the deed to your home. Assume your home is worth $100,000 at the time you add your children's names to the deed. When you add the children's name to the deed, you have made an irrevocable gift of $33,333.33 to each child. (You will need to read Chapter 18 to learn whether this will create a gift tax.) When you die, your children will each own a 50 percent interest in your home. Then, if one of your children dies, the home will belong 100 percent to the surviving child.

This may or may not be what you want. Some parents would want the children of a child who dies to have the property. This would not happen. The title to the home would automatically pass to the surviving child, even if the child who died had children.

Gift Tax Consequences

There are different gift tax consequences when a person creates a joint tenancy with his or her spouse, versus anyone else. When you create a joint tenancy with your spouse, there are no gift taxes. This is because you can give your spouse an unlimited amount of property without gift taxes. This is called an unlimited marital deduction.

When you create a joint tenancy with someone other than your spouse, you are making a gift that is subject to gift taxes. If you take a piece of property that is worth $100,000 and put the property in joint name with your son, you have made a $50,000 gift to your son. The only property you can place in joint name with someone who is not your spouse without generating a gift subject to gift taxes are bank accounts.

While we won't get into the particulars of gift taxes until Chapter 18, for now it is important to understand that when you create most joint tenancies with someone who is not your spouse, you are making an irrevocable gift that is subject to gift taxes. (E)

Chapter 11

Trusts Are
for Everyone

You don't have to be rich to enjoy the benefits of a trust. Nobody wants his or her family to spend money on lawyer fees that could have been avoided. When you understand the rules, you can have a trust prepared very cost-efficiently, and your family can enjoy the same benefits as rich people. This chapter will show you how.

What Is a Trust?

A trust is a legal document that allows you to maintain 100 percent control of your property while you are living. After you pass on, your trust can either transfer your property to your loved ones immediately or stay in place and distribute your property over time.

A trust involves three parties: the creator, the trustee, and the beneficiaries. What most people don't understand about a trust is that you can be all three parties while you are living. The fact that you wear all three hats allows you to control all of the decisions and puts a plan in place to distribute your property when you are gone.

Don't get confused by the terminology. You may have heard about living trusts, family trusts, marital trusts, insurance trusts, or revocable trusts. These are slang expressions that describe the purpose of that particular trust. In fact, all trusts have the same basic components.

The Creator

You are the creator of your trust. The creator of the trust is often referred to in legal terms as the *grantor* or the *settlor* of the trust. These are just different words to describe exactly the same thing. As the creator, you are going to make all the decisions about your trust. You will decide:

- What property is going to be transferred to your trust.
- Who will serve as trustee while you are living.
- Who will serve as trustee after you are gone.
- What the trustee will do with the property while you are living.
- Who will receive your property when you are gone.

After your trust document is complete, you will take the property you now own in your individual name and transfer ownership of the property into the name of the trustee. Most people name themselves as the initial trustee. It seems unnecessary, and even silly, to transfer ownership of your property from your name to your name as trustee, but keep reading. You'll see what happens.

The Trustee

When you create a trust, you need to name a trustee. The trustee will hold legal title to the property you transfer into the trust. You will usually name yourself as the initial trustee because you want to maintain control of your property. However, it is possible for you to name someone else to serve as the initial trustee if you are uncomfortable managing the property.

When you create your trust, you can name more than one initial trustee; they are called *co-trustees*. Sometimes a husband and wife will want to serve as co-trustees of each other's trust. This allows the spouses to continue to make joint decisions about the property that has been transferred to either of the trusts.

You also need to name a trustee who will become the trustee when the initial trustee is gone. This is called a *successor trustee*. You can have more than one successor trustee. Successor co-trustees are very common when parents are creating trusts and they have more than one child. Typically a parent creates his trust, names himself as initial trustee, then names his spouse to serve as successor trustee. But if both spouses are gone, the parent names his children to serve as successor co-trustees.

The Trustee Takes Control

When you can no longer serve as trustee, either because you have died or because you have become incapacitated, the person or entity you name as successor trustee automatically becomes the new trustee. It is like your successor steps into your shoes. When your successor trustee begins to serve, there is no change of ownership of the trust property and therefore your family does not need to probate your estate. Your trust owns all of your property. The trust just happens to have a new trustee after you are gone.

ALERT!

When you name all of your children as successor co-trustees, the children will have to agree on all of the decisions about your trust property. If your children can't make decisions together while you are living, don't expect them to develop this talent after you are gone.

Giving Instructions

Your next job as creator of your trust is to give your trustee instructions on what to do with your property. The instructions you put in your trust document typically have two parts. The first part of the instructions deals with what the trustee is required to do with the trust property while you are living. The second part of the instructions deals with what the successor trustee may or must do with the trust property after you are gone.

While you are living you can do all of the things with your property you could do before you created the trust. Your trust document will give the trustee, who is typically you, the power to:

- Change the trust document.
- Use all of the income from the property for whatever you want.
- Sell the trust property.
- Borrow against the trust property.
- Give the trust property away.

The second set of instructions you put in your trust document tells your successor trustee how and when to distribute your property. These are the hard decisions and the most important part of the trust document. Chapter 12 describes in detail the types of instructions you can include. After you read Chapter 12, you will be able to create a plan for your property to put in your trust document.

The Beneficiaries

Your trust document needs to establish who will receive your property. The person or persons who receive the benefits of the trust property are called *beneficiaries*. While you are living, you will probably name yourself as the beneficiary of your trust.

Most people know who they want to provide for, but don't understand the types of limitations that can be placed in a trust document to provide for the security of the beneficiaries. Chapter 12 explains your options. When you understand the types of powers you can give a successor trustee, and how you can limit the enjoyment of the property by your beneficiaries, it may actually change your mind about who you want to include in your plan. For instance, you may decide to include persons in your plan you otherwise wouldn't have because you can create conditions about what each person must do or not do to receive a distribution from your trust.

When you are the beneficiary of your trust, your trust document typically instructs the trustee, who is you, to distribute any of the trust property to you. Notice you are both the trustee and the beneficiary. Therefore, you are deciding what trust property to distribute to yourself. This is why you have control while you are living.

Powers of Appointment

While you are alive, you can change anything about your trust document, including the beneficiaries. While you are not available to make changes after you've passed, you can give someone else the power to change the beneficiaries. This is called a power of appointment. There are two types of powers of appointment: limited power of appointment and general power of appointment.

Limited Power of Appointment

A limited power of appointment is when you name someone in your trust document who has the power to appoint the trust property among a limited number of persons. This is a very important provision you should consider putting in your trust.

For example, assume you have a spouse and four children. You want your spouse to be the primary beneficiary of your trust after you are gone, and you want any property left in the trust after your spouse is gone to be distributed to your children. However, you may be reluctant to name your four children as equal beneficiaries. In which case, you can give your spouse a limited power of appointment to change the amount of property each of your four children will receive. Your spouse could live a long time after you are gone, and he or she may want to reward a child who is more helpful or even eliminate a child completely as a beneficiary.

The reason this power is called a limited power of appointment is because your spouse can only change the share each of your four children will receive. Your spouse can't remarry and leave all of your property to his or her new spouse, because the new spouse is not within the limited class you established in your trust, namely your four children.

General Power of Appointment

The second type of power is a general power of appointment. This allows the person to whom you give a general power of appointment to convey or appoint your property to anyone he so chooses.

Before you give anyone, even your spouse, a general power of appointment over your trust property after you are gone, you should understand that this person could change all of your beneficiaries and give your property to someone you might not have chosen as a beneficiary.

The persons you name as beneficiaries in your trust document will become irrevocable when you are gone, unless you have given someone a limited or a general power of appointment to change the beneficiaries.

Reasons for Creating a Trust

There are many reasons why you might want to create a trust. A trust allows you to control your property while you are living. If property is owned by your trust, it doesn't need to be probated when you die. A trust can save taxes. And a trust allows you to create a plan for your family.

Some of the reasons for having a trust may not apply to you. For instance, there are ways you can own your property, such as in joint name, that will allow your property to pass automatically to the surviving joint tenant without probate when you are gone. When you compare the advantages and disadvantages of owning property in joint name with the advantages and disadvantages of owning property in a trust, you may decide that you don't need a trust.

Perhaps you are not interested in a management plan for your property after you are gone. You may simply want your property distributed to specific persons and decide that even though it will be necessary to probate your property to transfer title to your loved ones, you only need a will to carry out your goals.

You could also learn that your estate will not owe any federal death taxes. Therefore, you do not need to create a trust to reduce your taxes.

Every family is different. This is why it is important to carefully consider the advantages and disadvantages of all plans to find the one that would best suit your wants and the needs of your loved ones.

Advantages of a Trust

There are many advantages to creating a trust. For example, your family can save money on probate and taxes, and you can put a more detailed plan in place to manage your property after you are gone. One of these advantages to creating a trust may be more important to your family than another.

Probate

One of the biggest advantages to creating a trust is that the property that is owned by your trust avoids the probate process after you are gone. When you create a trust, you usually name yourself as the initial trustee. You transfer the property you want owned by the trust to yourself as trustee. You name a successor trustee in your trust document. The successor trustee automatically owns the property when you are gone, thus avoiding the probate process. This is a huge advantage. It is not only expensive for your family to probate your estate after you are gone, but it is also frustrating.

FACT

When you serve as trustee while you are living, about the only thing that has changed for you by creating a trust is that your property is not owned by you as an individual, but is owned by you as trustee for your own benefit.

Control

Creating a trust lets you maintain 100 percent control of your property while you are living and be certain that your property will be controlled the way you want after you are gone. As creator of the trust, you make all the decisions about what instructions you want included in your trust document. Because you typically serve as your own trustee while you are alive, you hold legal title to your property and continue to control your property. You, as the trustee, are the only one who has the power to sell the trust property, borrow against the trust property, and manage the property in your trust. You are also the beneficiary while you are living. This means that you have all of the income and benefits from the property.

Management

This is an advantage that is not available with any other type of estate-planning document. Your trust document has detailed instructions on who will manage your property after you are gone or if you become incapacitated. The successor trustee you name will automatically hold the legal title to your trust property. Your trust document will provide instructions to your successor trustee on what to do with that property.

The instructions you give your successor trustee might be very simple and straightforward. For instance, the trust could say, "My successor trustee shall distribute all of the trust property to my spouse," or "My successor trustee shall, if my spouse and I are both gone, distribute my trust property in equal shares to my children." If this is your plan, the only advantage you have gained by creating a trust is that of saving your family the cost and delay associated with the probate process.

When you read Chapter 12 and discover the types of powers and discretion you can give your successor trustee, you will be surprised. You may consider creating a trust even if you thought your property and estate plan was very simple.

Taxes

It is important that you determine whether your estate will be subject to federal death taxes after you and your spouse are gone. Federal death taxes are very expensive. (Chapter 18 will tell you how to compute your federal death tax exposure.)

If you are married and you and your spouse own property in excess of the amount that can be transferred free of federal death taxes, you can use trusts that include special tax-savings provisions to save your family $345,800 in federal death taxes. (The language you need to put in your trusts to save federal death taxes is described in Chapter 19.)

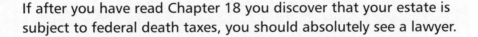

ALERT! If after you have read Chapter 18 you discover that your estate is subject to federal death taxes, you should absolutely see a lawyer.

Disadvantages of a Trust

The main disadvantage to creating a trust is that it takes you quite a bit of time to get organized and make the decisions needed. It is also more expensive to create a trust than it is to create a will. However, if you understand the rules, are organized, and have made all of the necessary decisions, the cost of creating a trust will be substantially reduced.

Time and Expense

The reason it is more expensive to create a trust than a will is because you need to transfer ownership of each piece of property from your name to your name as the trustee of the trust. Earlier, it was recommended that you begin the planning process by purchasing a three-ring binder or notebook. Take a look at how many different sheets of paper you have describing each individual piece of property. By flipping through your notebook, you can evaluate how expensive it will be to transfer ownership of your property to your trust. However, you may be pleasantly surprised to discover that you can transfer ownership of most of your property without the help of a lawyer. If you have described each piece of property you own on a separate piece of paper, you should write the following question on each: "How do I transfer title to this piece of property?"

Transferring Real Estate

If you own real estate, you need a deed to transfer the real estate from your name, or from joint name, to your name as trustee of your trust. It is highly recommend that you do not try to prepare your own deed—there are too many ways you can make a mistake. If you have a copy of your current deed, unless there is something complicated or unusual about your real estate, it should not cost more than $75 per deed to have a lawyer prepare a new deed to transfer the real estate to your name as trustee of your trust.

Transferring Bank Accounts

Most of your bank accounts can be changed into your name as trustee by completing a form with the bank. Sometimes the bank will require that you close the existing account and open a new one in your name as trustee of your trust. This can be a time-consuming hassle, but it is not something you need to hire a lawyer to do. The bank may also require a copy of your trust document.

ESSENTIAL

If you have a brokerage account, ask if you can change the name on the account to your name as trustee of your trust. Again, you may have to open a new brokerage account. Though time-consuming, it isn't a difficult task.

Transferring Stock Shares

If you own shares of stock in your individual name, it is going to be almost impossible to change the name on your stock certificates. You should open a brokerage account in your name as trustee. Some brokerage firms will complete the paperwork free of charge to transfer the individual shares from your name to your new brokerage account.

Transferring Life Insurance, Annuities, and Retirement Accounts

If you own life insurance or annuities or have retirement accounts, you are going to need to understand the rules about each of these individual investments before you decide whether you want your trust to be the beneficiary or owner of these types of assets. Each asset has its own chapter that will help you make the decision.

If you understand what a trust is and have made the necessary decisions, it should not take your lawyer much more time to prepare a trust document than it would take him or her to prepare a will.

Even though it takes time to transfer your assets to your name as trustee of your trust, imagine how expensive it is for your survivors to transfer title after you are gone. And if your property was in your name, your loved ones will have to pay a lawyer to obtain the approval of the probate court to make the same transfers after you are gone.

Chapter 12

Decisions to Include Within a Trust

This chapter will help you understand the types of powers you can give your successor trustee and the conditions you can place on your beneficiaries. There are a lot of decisions to be made and it can be time-consuming, but you will end up with a trust that accomplishes your goals and meets the needs of your loved ones.

Your Choice of Recipients

Chapter 2 guided you through a process of deciding who should receive your property, what the person should receive, when your property should be distributed and why. You were encouraged to develop a miniplan for each person. However, when you learn about the flexibility of trusts and the types of decisions you can make for your family, you may find yourself revising those pieces of paper.

Most people know who they want to provide for in their estate plan. It is also fair to say that even when you know who you would like to include in your plan, you often have concerns about what will happen. You may have some of the following concerns:

- How should you divide your property?
- What is fair?
- Is this a second marriage for you?
- Do you want your surviving spouse to have complete control over your property after you are gone?
- What will happen if your child divorces?
- Are you concerned that your daughter- or son-in-law will take your child's inheritance?
- Do any of your beneficiaries have special needs?
- Will your beneficiaries squander their inheritance?

If any of these issues concern you, you need to continue reading to learn how you can create a trust that can relieve your concerns.

ESSENTIAL

You are going to learn about the types of powers and discretion you can give to your successor trustee. If you create a trust that is going to be in existence for many years after you are gone, it may change your decisions about how you want to distribute your property.

When Your Property Is Distributed

Your trust document can instruct your successor trustee to distribute your property immediately or to make delayed distributions. As you continue to read this chapter, you will probably develop both a short-term and long-term budget for your beneficiaries.

Current Distributions

If all of your property is in your trust, you need to give your successor trustee the power to make current distributions after you are gone. Even if you don't want to do this, state law will force your successor trustee to use your trust property to pay your outstanding unpaid bills, debts, and taxes if you had the power to alter, amend, or revoke your trust document while you were living, which is common for most people if they want to maintain control of their property.

In addition to giving your successor trustee the power to pay your bills, debts, and taxes, you typically want to give him or her the power to make current distributions of cash or property, because your beneficiaries will need money within a reasonable time after you are gone. How much your beneficiaries will need is different for all families.

Alternatively, you may simply want all of your property distributed as soon as possible after your death. If this is your plan, you will instruct your successor trustee to distribute your property to your named beneficiaries as soon as the trustee provides for the payment of your outstanding bills and taxes.

Delayed Distributions

One of the primary reasons people create trusts is to delay distributions to their beneficiaries. There are some limits on how long you can delay the distributions from your trust, and all states have different laws regarding this length of time. For instance, some states won't allow you to postpone the final distribution from your trust longer than twenty-one years after a "life in being." This is the classic rule against perpetuities. In the states following the classic rule against perpetuities, if you had a great-grandchild who is living and the beneficiary of your trust, all the trust property must be distributed within twenty-one years after the death of the great-grandchild.

FACT

The rule against perpetuities is so complex that many states changed to a rule that says that your trust property must be distributed within ninety-nine years after your death.

It is very typical to delay trust distributions until a beneficiary has reached a particular age. Unless you are trying to delay distributions for multiple generations, there are very few limits on how you can structure the distributions of your trust property. Some people think that a beneficiary should not receive property until he or she is twenty-five years old, others feel thirty is the magic age, and still others want to make sure their beneficiaries plan for their retirement, and therefore distributions to the beneficiaries are restricted until he or she reaches the age of fifty-five or sixty years old!

Triggering Events

You can put triggering events into your trust document. A triggering event is something that must happen before the beneficiary is entitled to receive a distribution of trust money or property. Likewise, you can put in your trust document triggering events that might cause the termination of trust distributions of money or property.

ALERT!

Be careful: When you put restrictions in your trust document that determine whether your beneficiary receives one or more trust distributions, you have put your trustee in the position of being a watchdog.

For instance, if you put in your trust document that the successor trustee must distribute $1/3$ of the trust property to the beneficiary when the beneficiary reaches the age of twenty-five, reaching the age of twenty-five is a triggering event. It would not matter how badly your beneficiary might need the trust property when he or she is twenty-three years old; the successor trustee cannot distribute cash or property until the beneficiary reaches the triggering age of twenty-five.

You can be even more disciplinary about your triggering events. For example, you may stipulate that your beneficiary will receive $1/3$ of the trust property when she graduates from college with at least a B average. If she graduates from college with a C+ average, she will not receive the distribution. Or, if your beneficiary does not graduate from college at all, she will not receive the distribution.

Restrictions and Penalties

Some people want to include a triggering event that is a penalty. For instance, you could state that if your beneficiary ever smokes cigarettes, the distributions he or she is receiving will stop.

A restriction that many people are putting in their trust documents is to require the spouse of a beneficiary to execute a release of any interest the spouse may have in the beneficiary's trust property. This helps protect your trust assets in the event a beneficiary divorces.

ESSENTIAL

Keep in mind, if you put restrictions in your trust document, you have more decisions to make. If a beneficiary is going to lose his or her trust distributions or does not qualify to receive the trust distributions because the conditions were not met, you need to include instructions in your trust document telling your successor trustee what he or she should do with the forfeited property.

You can put any restrictions or triggering event in your trust document that are not illegal or contrary to public policy. For instance, you cannot direct your successor trustee to make a distribution if the beneficiary commits an illegal act, such as "the beneficiary receives $1,000 when he robs the local convenience store." Examples of restrictions that violate public policy are not as definitive. Public policy issues typically involve restricting your beneficiary's choice of religion, freedom to associate, right to vote, and other things of this nature.

A public policy issue that is common is restricting a beneficiary's right to marry. If you place a restriction in the trust document such as "The beneficiary won't receive any trust distributions if he marries before he is twenty-five years old," this has been deemed a reasonable restriction. However, if you limit the class of persons your beneficiary can marry, this is typically considered a restriction that will violate public policy and will not be enforced.

How Your Property Should Be Distributed

When you think about how your property should be distributed, it may affect what each beneficiary will receive. If you instruct your trustee to divide your property equally among your beneficiaries, such as your children, he must decide who gets what. He will consult with your beneficiaries regarding how to divide your trust property, but if your beneficiaries disagree, any of them can petition your local probate court to resolve the controversy. When the beneficiaries argue about the trust property, the probate court becomes involved, lawyers need to be hired, and things get expensive. This outcome can be avoided if you provide more specific instructions to your successor trustee.

There are three types of instructions you can give a trustee: specific instructions, general instructions, or a blend of specific and general instructions. The types of instructions you put in your trust document will depend on the nature of the management plan you are creating for your beneficiaries.

Most people think that if they have a trust, the property in the trust will avoid the probate process. This is true as long as there are no disagreements among the beneficiaries.

The first thing you need to understand is that your trustee has no choice but to follow the instructions you put in your trust document.

Specific instructions can be a one-time instruction or continuing instructions. It depends on how long you want your trust to remain in place after you are gone.

Specific One-Time Instructions

Specific one-time instructions are typically included in a trust document because the trust is going to terminate shortly after you are gone or there are certain immediate distributions you want your successor trustee to make. You could list all of your property and give your trustee specific instructions on how to distribute the trust property. For example, you could instruct your trustee to distribute:

- My two-carat diamond ring to my daughter
- My Rolex watch to my son
- My ABC brokerage account to my son
- My XYS savings account to my daughter
- My 1999 Saab to my son

If you took the time to give your trustee specific instructions about each piece of property you own, the trustee would have no discretion. This is a rather unrealistic example because it would be almost impossible to create a trust document that describes every single piece of property you own. You would need to change your trust document every time you bought something!

Specific instructions are also commonly included in a trust document when you want to include persons or organizations as beneficiaries who are not your family members. For example, you may instruct your successor trustee to distribute $50,000 to your friend Mary Smith and $10,000 to your church.

Continuing Specific Instructions

Continuing specific instructions are included in a trust document when you want to provide money or property to a beneficiary over a period of time, but you don't want to put the successor trustee in a position of deciding how much money or property should be distributed. The specific continuing instructions can be a stated amount of money or a percentage of the trust. For example, you can instruct your successor trustee to distribute $1,000 per month to your beneficiary until the beneficiary reaches age twenty-five. Or you can instruct your trustee to distribute 5 percent of the value of the trust to your beneficiary each year for a period of twenty years.

FACT

There are any number of reasons you may choose continuing specific distributions. For instance, perhaps you don't trust that your beneficiary will make the right decisions if he or she receives too much property at one time. Or you may want to make sure that if your spouse dies, the remaining trust property will be distributed to your children and not the beneficiaries of your spouse.

General Instructions

General instructions are when you give the successor trustee the power to exercise his or her discretion in deciding how much or when to make a distribution from your trust. While you are living and serving as the trustee, your trust document typically gives you 100 percent discretion to do anything you want with the trust property. You can create your trust document where you give the successor trustee as much discretion as you had when you were alive. Most people would only consider giving this amount of discretion to a successor trustee when he or she is the spouse, and the beneficiaries are the spouse and the natural children of both spouses.

ALERT!

If you give this amount of discretion to your spouse as your successor trustee, you may be subjecting your spouse's estate to federal death taxes that could have been avoided had you not given your spouse such broad discretion. See Chapter 18 for further details.

Specific and General Instructions Combined

There are instructions you can give your successor trustee that are a blend of specific instructions and general instructions. The most common example of a blended instruction is to instruct your successor trustee to make any distributions to a beneficiary that she or he believes the beneficiary needs for a particular purpose. The purpose you define can be narrow or broad. A broad blended instruction would be to instruct your successor trustee to distribute such amount of money or property for health, education, maintenance, or welfare. Although this instruction is broad and gives your successor trustee a great deal of discretion, he or she cannot make distributions that are not necessary for health, education, maintenance, or welfare. If your beneficiary wants to buy a $100,000 car, your trustee can refuse the request for funds because the car does not fall under one of the specified categories.

You may decide that you want to give your successor trustee general instructions, but you want to limit his or her discretion. You could put in your trust document that the successor trustee is to distribute $1,000 per month, plus any amount of money he or she feels the beneficiary needs for health or education. Now you have given your successor trustee a specific instruction as well as a general instruction. It is difficult for a beneficiary to argue that he or she needs money to buy a car or take a vacation when the instructions to the successor trustee are that additional money can be distributed only for health or education.

FACT

If your instructions are specific, and the successor trustee fails to make the required distribution, the beneficiary is entitled to petition the local probate court to force the successor trustee to distribute the withheld money or property.

You could give your successor trustee an intentionally vague instruction. For example, "My trustee shall pay for all housing costs for the beneficiary." This leaves the window open for the beneficiary to demand a large amount for housing. If you wanted a little more restriction, you could have instructed your successor trustee to distribute a reasonable amount to the beneficiary for housing costs. There is still room to argue about the magic word *reasonable,* but it adds some restrictions on what the successor trustee can distribute for housing, and therefore limits what the beneficiary can demand.

The Power to Sell Your Property

A trust document should always include a section defining the powers of the trustee. While you are serving as trustee, you typically want the document to give you the power to change the trust document, revoke the trust document, and to manage the property in the same fashion you could have managed the property when it was in your individual name. But when you are gone, you need to decide what powers you are going to give your successor trustee.

Defining the Trustee's Power

restriction on rental?

Typically, you do not want the successor trustee to be able to change the core decisions about your plan. Therefore, you should define what powers she or he will have regarding the management of the trust property. Your successor trustee is usually given all of the powers any property manager would have, such as the power to invest, reinvest, borrow, rent, or improve the property. Notice that these standard powers will give your successor trustee the power to sell your property.

FACT

It is difficult to have a trust stay in existence for very long after you are gone if the successor trustee is not given the power to sell the trust property. The economy changes, and the successor trustee needs to be able to effectively manage the property.

Placing Restrictions on the Selling of Property

If you do not want one or more pieces of your trust property sold, you need to include a restriction in the trust document prohibiting the successor trustee from selling that piece of property. You may not want the trustee to be prevented from selling an asset forever, but merely for a period of time. This is a common restriction used when a parent wants the trustee to keep her home until her children reach a particular age.

The Power to Sell as an Incentive

Alternatively, you may use the power to sell as an incentive to keep your beneficiaries from arguing. If your trust document directs the successor trustee to divide the trust property among your beneficiaries, you might consider including an instruction in your trust document that says if the beneficiaries do not agree on how the trust property will be divided and distributed within a certain amount of time, the trustee is instructed to sell the property and divide the proceeds. This type of instruction often serves two purposes: It motivates the beneficiaries to reach an agreement, and it prevents your beneficiaries from filing a complaint with the local probate court if they cannot agree.

Chapter 13

Choosing a Trustee

People create trusts for different reasons. Some people create a trust because the nature and extent of their property is so complicated that they need professional management. Others create a trust because they simply want to avoid probate. Your motivation for creating a trust is going to have a significant impact on whom you choose as trustee.

Sequence of Trustees

There is a sequence of three trustees in most trust documents. There is the initial trustee who serves while you are living, typically yourself. Then, you need to name a successor trustee who will serve after you are gone. And finally, you should name a second successor trustee to serve if the first successor you name is not available.

The Initial Trustee

As you know, most people name themselves as the initial trustee; however, this isn't always the case. You might name someone else to serve as the initial trustee because you are nervous about managing your own property. This could be because your health is failing, or your property is sufficiently complicated that you feel someone else could better manage it. If the latter applies to you, you should consider naming a professional trustee.

There are numerous options for you to choose from if you want a professional trustee. The best place to look is your local bank. Most banks maintain a trust department. The nice thing about this choice is that your local bank controls your accounts, and it makes it easier for them to be of service to you. If you don't want to use your bank, there are trust companies whose sole function is to manage trust assets and act as trustees. Most brokerage companies can also serve as trustee for you. The advantage of naming a professional trustee is that your assets are professionally managed.

You usually name yourself as the initial trustee because you want to maintain 100 percent control of your property, and you feel you are competent to manage it. But there is no rule that says you have to.

Successor Trustee

The second in the sequence of trustees is called a successor trustee. This is the person or entity that will serve as successor trustee when the initial trustee is not available to serve. When you serve as your own initial trustee, there must be a successor trustee who can serve after you are gone.

Deciding who will be your successor trustee is not easy. However, this chapter will guide you through the duties and responsibilities of a trustee, which should help you to make the important decision.

Second Successor Trustee

The third in the sequence of trustees is still called a successor trustee, but it is the second successor trustee. This is the person or entity that will serve as trustee if your first successor trustee is not available.

If you name a professional trustee like a bank, a trust company, or a brokerage firm to serve as your initial trustee, you don't need to name a successor trustee because the professional trustee won't die or become unavailable to serve.

Duties of the Trustee

Your trustee has two duties. He or she must manage the trust property and distribute the trust property to the beneficiaries. When you create your trust you put two sets of instructions in your trust document. The first set of instructions deals with how to manage the trust property, and the second set deals with what the trustee is supposed to do with the trust property for the benefit of the beneficiaries.

Management of the Trust Property

There are two duties your trustee has regarding the management of your trust property. The first duty of the trustee is to follow the instructions you have provided in the trust document. Those regarding the management of the trust property are typically boilerplate instructions.

Most trust documents give the trustee very broad management powers. If you don't want your trustee to be able to exercise a particular management power over the trust property, you need to restrict her or him from having that power. For instance, some creators of trusts do not want to give the trustee the power to borrow against the property. Be aware, however, that if your trust is going to stay in place for a long time after you are gone, it is very difficult for your trustee to manage the trust property if you place too many restrictions on what he or she can do with the trust property.

ALERT!

When you restrict the power of your trustee to manage your property, you could be hurting the value of the property to the detriment of your beneficiaries.

If your trust is not going to last very long, it may be important to you that the trust property is not sold. Your goal may be to delay the distribution of the trust property until the beneficiaries are older. In that case, prohibiting the trustee from selling trust property may meet your goals. You need to first consider the purpose of your trust, and then decide how or if you want to restrict the management powers of the trustee.

Duty Established by Law

Regardless of the specific instructions you place in your trust document, your trustee has a duty that is established by law. Your trustee must manage the trust property as a reasonably prudent person would do. There are two different standards for this. Some state laws say that the trustee must manage the trust property as a reasonably prudent person would do if he or she were managing his or her own property. Other states say that the trustee must manage the trust property as a reasonably prudent person would do if he or she were managing the property of another. Believe it or not, it is supposed to be a higher standard of care when you are managing the property of another person. Either way, the trustee has a duty to be careful in his or her decisions on how the trust property is managed.

If the person you choose as your successor trustee is not very sophis-ticated with making decisions about money or investments, you could be subjecting that person to being sued by the beneficiaries, even though he or she was doing the best job possible under the circumstances. This is a particularly dangerous possibility if you name your spouse as successor trustee and you have children from a previous marriage. For instance, let's

say you name your second spouse as successor trustee, and you name
your children from a former marriage as beneficiaries of your trust assets
after your second spouse is gone. If the trust assets go down in value, your
children may become angry and sue your spouse for not managing the
trust assets in a reasonably prudent manner.

FACT

If the trustee is not reasonably prudent with the trust property,
your beneficiaries have a right to have the trustee removed and/or
to sue the trustee. If your beneficiaries sue the trustee, they can
recover the losses caused to the trust property from the trustee's
personal assets. However, it is difficult and expensive for your
beneficiaries to win such a lawsuit.

Duties to the Beneficiaries

As you know, your trustee must follow the specific instructions you
have put in your trust document. But if you choose to give your trustee
discretion regarding what trust property to distribute or when to make the
distributions, your trustee must exercise his or her discretionary powers in
a reasonably prudent manner. The more specific your instructions are,
the easier it will be for your trustee to follow those instructions.

Important Considerations

There are several factors you should consider when choosing a trustee:

- How long will your trust remain in place after you are gone?
- How complex will it be for your trustee to manage the trust property?
- What is the relationship between the proposed successor trustee and
  your beneficiaries?
- Do any of your beneficiaries have special needs?

People create trusts for different reasons. When you name an
individual to serve as your trustee, you should be confident that the

person you name has the skills to serve and will follow the instructions in your trust document.

If your trustee is going to distribute the trust assets to your beneficiaries shortly after you are gone, you can choose a successor trustee who is efficient, well-organized, and able to handle the paperwork to make the distributions. But if your trust is going to exist for many years after you are gone, it becomes more challenging to choose a successor trustee.

If the property that will be owned by your trust is complex, you should choose a successor trustee who has the skills to manage that type of property. If you have given your trustee a great deal of discretion about when and how to make distributions to your beneficiaries, it may be more important that you name a trustee who will understand the emotional needs of your beneficiaries.

Relationship Considerations

You should also consider the successor trustee's relationship to the beneficiaries. If you name your spouse as successor trustee, and the spouse is not the natural parent of your children—who are also benefi-ciaries—there is greater possibility for conflict. If you are creating a trust where your children are the beneficiaries, and you name one child to act as your successor trustee for the benefit of your other children, there can be hard feelings between the child you chose and your other children. This can be particularly troublesome if the child who is serving as your successor trustee is also a beneficiary of your trust.

More Than One Trustee

You can have more than one trustee. When you have more than one trustee, they are called co-trustees. Naming more than one trustee might alleviate some of the concerns you might have about trying to decide who should serve as your trustee.

For instance, if the property owned by your trust is complex, but you want the personal touch, you might consider naming a person you trust to make the right personal decisions for your beneficiaries as one co-trustee and a professional as the second co-trustee. The co-trustees will make the decisions together, and this can provide the best of both worlds for your beneficiaries.

> The more careful you are about creating your plan and choosing the right trustee, the more likely your plan will be successful and accomplish the goals you want achieved for your family.

Naming a professional co-trustee may not be a financially realistic option for you. All professional trustees charge a fee for serving. There is typically a minimum annual fee plus a charge computed as a percentage of all of the assets owned by the trust. The percentage ranges from ¾ of 1 percent to 2 or 3 percent, depending on the value of all of the trust assets. You may want a professional trustee, but it could be cost-prohibitive given the total value of your trust assets.

You don't have to name a professional to act as your co-trustee. You may have two children whom you feel would bring different talents to the job. Therefore, you name both children to act as co-trustees. You need to make sure that the two persons you name can work together. Unless you specify differently in your trust document, the co-trustees must make all decisions together.

There is no limit to the number of co-trustees you can name in your trust document. You could name three, four, or even more co-trustees. However, there does come a point where it isn't practical to expect the co-trustees to make decisions when there are too many fingers in the pie. You know the old saying, too many cooks spoil the broth.

The Trustee and Your Property

As stated before, there are two things the trustee must do with your trust property. He or she must manage the trust property with reasonable care and follow the instructions you have put in the trust document. When you create your trust, you will define the management powers of your trustee.

Selling the Property

There are several reasons you might prohibit your trustee from selling your property. For instance, it might be your goal to keep the trust property in the family, but you want to make sure the beneficiaries are old enough to properly care for the property. Therefore, you place the property in trust and instruct the trustee to distribute it to your beneficiaries at a later time. Or you may feel that it is the best choice to make sure the trust property is not sold for a period of time, because you feel that particular property will provide the best income or security for your beneficiaries.

If you don't want your trustee to be able to sell your property, you need to include an instruction in your trust document that prohibits your trustee from doing so. When you restrict this power, you could be hurting the value of the property to the detriment of your beneficiaries. But if your trust is not going to last that long, it may be important to you that the trust property is not sold. Of course, these are decisions only you can make.

ALERT!

You need to be careful when you prohibit a trustee from selling the trust property. If circumstances change and it would be better to sell the property, the trustee cannot do so under any circumstances, because your trust document instructed the trustee that he or she could not sell.

Dividing Your Property

Whether or not your property is physically divided depends on the instructions you put in your trust document. Some types of property can be easily divided. If your goal is to make certain a beneficiary receives a portion of a specific piece of property, instruct the trustee not to sell the property, but to physically divide the trust property among the beneficiaries.

Remember those sheets of paper that describe each piece of property you own? You can make notes on the pieces of paper about whether you would like to instruct the trustee to sell that piece of property, divide the property among your beneficiaries, or distribute it to a particular beneficiary.

The more thought you put into the instructions you give your trustee about your property, the less likely it is your beneficiaries will disagree after you are gone.

If Your Family Doesn't Agree

If the beneficiaries of your trust do not agree with what the trustee is doing, they may file a lawsuit. The beneficiaries will file papers with the court explaining to the judge why the trustee is making, or is about to make, a bad decision about your trust property. Lawsuits are expensive. The beneficiary who is dissatisfied will need to hire a lawyer, the trustee will need to hire a lawyer, and often the other beneficiaries who will be affected will need to hire a lawyer. If three lawyers are involved, it could cost $600 or more per hour to resolve the dispute!

There are two solutions: You can be very specific in your trust document about what each beneficiary will receive, though this may not be practical if your trust is going to remain in place for a long time. Or you can put a provision in your trust document that says if the beneficiaries disagree about how the trust property is going to be divided and distributed, the trustee is to sell the property and divide the proceeds. This instruction gives the trustee the authority to solve the dispute, rather than the local courts.

Even after the beneficiaries and the trustee present their side of the argument to the judge, if your instructions were not clear or there were no specific instructions, the judge will often order the property sold and divide the proceeds among the beneficiaries.

Financial Guardian for Your Minor Child

There are two types of guardianships for a minor child: legal guardian and financial guardian. As you know, the legal guardian is the physical guardian of your child. A trust can name a financial guardian for your minor child, but it cannot name a legal guardian.

If you create a trust for your minor child, your successor trustee in essence becomes the financial guardian of that child. The successor trustee will follow the instructions you put in the trust document about how to manage and distribute your property for the benefit of the child.

When people divorce, they often overlook the fact that if they die and leave their assets to their minor child, the surviving natural parent becomes the physical guardian and also controls the assets they've left to the child. You can prevent your ex-spouse from having control of your children's money and property by placing your assets in trust and naming a successor trustee whom you are confident will manage and spend the money only for the benefit of your child.

FACT

Your will is the only document that allows you to name a physical guardian for your minor child. Chapter 7 covered the specifics about what you should include in your will regarding appointment of a guardian for your minor child.

Even when parents are not divorced, both parents could die in a common accident. Therefore, you may want to create a will to name a person who will be physical guardian of your minor child, but create a trust that names a successor trustee to manage the property for that child.

Chapter 14

Creating a Trust

It is now time for you to see a real trust. As you review each section of the trust document, you will see the decisions Jane made for her family, and how she incorporated her plan into her trust document. You can use this sample document as a roadmap to create a trust for your family.

Identify the Parties and Describe the Property

Trust documents are broken into parts. Each part of a trust document accomplishes a purpose that is typically described by the title of the article. Besides the legalese, a trust document reads like a book. Each chapter covers a different topic. The first part identifies the parties and describes the property involved.

JANE ADAMS DOE
REVOCABLE TRUST AGREEMENT

I, JANE ADAMS DOE, a resident of Sarasota, Florida, do hereby enter into the JANE ADAMS DOE REVOCABLE TRUST between myself as Settlor and myself as Trustee.

Jane has identified herself as the one entering into the trust (the creator) and she has identified herself as the initial trustee.

ARTICLE I
ESTABLISHMENT OF TRUST

1.1 <u>Name of Trust.</u> This Trust may be referred to as the JANE ADAMS DOE REVOCABLE TRUST.

In **ARTICLE 1.1**, Jane gives her trust a name, the "JANE ADAMS DOE REVOCABLE TRUST." You can give your trust any name. For instance, Jane could have called her revocable trust the "Mickey Mouse Trust." However, if your trust is going to own your property while you are alive, and you are going to be the initial trustee, it is best not to create confusion by giving your trust an unusual name.

1.2 <u>Declarations.</u> I am a married woman. My husband is JOHN ALEXANDER DOE. I have two (2) children: JACK JOSEPH DOE and

JAMIE ANN DOE. Except as otherwise qualified, the words "child" or "children" when used in this Agreement with reference to me shall mean all my above-named children. The words "child" or "children" when used in this Agreement with reference to any person other than me shall mean all natural and adopted children including natural children born after the death of their parent but excluding stepchildren and foster children. The word "descendants" when used in this Agreement shall mean all of the person's lineal descendants of all generations, except those who are descendants of a living descendant, with the relationship of parent and child at each generation being determined under governing law. To be a child or descendant by virtue of adoption, the person must be adopted while a minor.

ARTICLE 1.2 is the declaration portion of the trust. You should list all the persons who are going to be beneficiaries of your trust and define the relationship of those persons to you. If you are going to name brothers, sisters, friends, or neighbors as beneficiaries, describe the people and their relationship to you.

1.3 <u>Trust Corpus.</u> I hereby transfer and deliver the property listed on Schedule A. All trust property shall be held by the Trustee in trust as is provided in this Agreement.

ARTICLE 1.3 declares that you are going to attach Schedule A to describe the property owned by the trust. It is very important for you to understand that listing the property as owned by the trust does not automatically make the property owned by the trust. You must change the ownership of the property from yourself to your trustee, even if you are serving as the initial trustee. If the trustee does not own the property, the trust will have no effect on how your property is distributed.

1.4 <u>Additional Trust Property.</u> From time to time I or any other person(s) may individually or jointly transfer additional property to this Trust or to any separate trust established hereunder. Additions of property may be made from any source by assignment, conveyance, or delivery, or by any testamentary disposition or appointment. Additions of life insurance policy proceeds or other monies payable on death may be made by designation of the Trustee as a beneficiary thereof.

ARTICLE 1.4 gives the trustee the power to accept property from other persons or sources. For instance, perhaps your parents are doing their estate planning. You could have their estate-planning documents leave property to the trustee of your trust, rather than directly to you. Remember, one of the goals of your trust is for your family to avoid probate after you are gone. Your property must be titled in the name of the trust to accomplish that goal.

Assigning the Power to Control the Trust Property

This is the part of your trust document that gives you 100 percent control of the trust property. You as the creator of the trust document are keeping the power to change or revoke the trust without anyone's approval.

ARTICLE II
RESERVATIONS

2.1 <u>Amendment and Revocation.</u> I may, during my lifetime and without the consent of anyone, revoke this Agreement in whole or in part (whereupon the trust property or the part affected by such revocation shall be distributed in accordance with my instructions) or amend it from time to time in any respect.

ARTICLE III
LIFETIME MANAGEMENT

3.1 <u>Income.</u> The Trustee shall pay to me the net income, if any, in such installments and amounts as I direct. In the absence of such direction, net income not distributed shall be accumulated and become part of the principal.

3.2 <u>Invasion of Principal.</u> The Trustee shall have the discretionary power to pay me such principal as will, when combined with my other income, support and maintain me so that I might, as near as possible with due regard to my total estate and my future financial requirements for myself and my dependents known to the Trustee, continue to enjoy the standard of living to which I am accustomed. This power shall be liberally construed without regard to remaindermen's interests and shall also include amounts for the care, support, education, medical and dental care, and general welfare and well-being of persons dependent on me, premiums on life insurance on my life whether or not such policies are assigned to or payable to the Trustee, and all sums necessary to preserve and protect my property.

ARTICLE III directs the trustee, who is probably you, to pay you, the beneficiary while you are alive, all of the income and any principal you need or want. If you have named someone else as the initial trustee, you are instructing that trustee to distribute any income or principal you request. The trustee cannot say no.

ARTICLE IV
CONSEQUENCES OF DEATH

4.1 <u>Death.</u> At my death this Agreement shall be irrevocable. The Trustee shall receive and hold as part of this Trust all then remaining principal and undistributed net income as well as any proceeds of any insurance on my life and all other property received by the Trustee at my death or at any time thereafter from any source. After my death the Trustee shall administer and distribute this Trust in accordance with the provisions of Article V.

ARTICLE IV makes the trust irrevocable when you die. The person or entity you name as your successor trustee will automatically become the new trustee, and Article 5 will now control what the successor trustee does with the trust property.

Timing and Distribution of Assets

When you review **ARTICLE V** you will see that Jane has given her successor trustee different instructions for different beneficiaries. Your plan does not have to be the same for all of your beneficiaries. The flexibility to create different plans for each beneficiary is one of the features that makes a trust a very attractive estate-planning document.

ARTICLE V

DURATION AND DISTRIBUTION OF TRUST

5.1 <u>Trust Share and Taxes, Debts, and Expenses.</u> The Trustee may pay from the Trust all federal estate taxes, including any interest or penalties thereon, for which my estate shall be liable. The Trustee shall also pay from the Trust such of the inheritance, estate, succession, transfer, and other death taxes, both federal and state, including any interest or penalties thereon, charged against my estate or any person or entity, which become payable by reason of my death, whether in respect to property passing under this Trust, my Will or otherwise. If there is no probate estate and therefore no Personal Representative of my estate, the Trustee shall pay such taxes and, in addition, all debts, expenses of my last illness, expenses of my funeral, burial, cemetery marker, cremation, or other disposition of my body, administration expenses and all other expenses and charges of a similar nature that the Trustee determines are a proper charge against my estate.

ARTICLE 5.1 instructs your successor trustee to pay all of your debts, final expenses, and any taxes you or your estate may owe after you are gone, even if there is no probate. If you have done your homework and put the title to all of your property that would have been subject to probate in the name of your trust, there will be no probate. That is why your successor trustee needs authority to pay your debts and expenses.

5.2 <u>Distribution for the Benefit of My Husband, JOHN ALEXANDER DOE.</u> If my husband, JOHN ALEXANDER DOE, is living, the rest and remainder of the accumulated income and principal shall be distributed to JOHN ALEXANDER DOE, Trustee of the JOHN ALEXANDER DOE REVOCABLE TRUST.

The instructions you give your successor trustee about how to distribute the trust property after you are gone is the meat and potatoes of your trust document. Jane created a trust where her successor trustee is instructed to distribute all of her trust property to her husband's trust when she dies. Jane must have been satisfied that John's trust included a plan for any property his trust receives from her trust. Jane and John probably calculated whether John's estate would be exposed to federal death taxes if Jane died first and

John's trust ended up owning all of the marital property. If the combined property would create a federal death tax, the trust provisions described in Chapter 19 should be considered to reduce the federal death tax exposure.

Jane could have created her trust differently. Jane's trust could have instructed the trustee to distribute income only to John, instructed the trustee to distribute a stated amount of cash annually to John, given her successor trustee the power to evaluate and distribute what John needed, or included a provision in her trust that John receives distributions only as long as he does not remarry.

5.3 <u>Distribution If My Husband, JOHN ALEXANDER DOE, Is Not Living.</u> If my husband, JOHN ALEXANDER DOE, is not living, the accumulated income and principal shall be distributed as follows:

5.3(a) <u>Trust for the Benefit of My Son, JACK JOSEPH DOE.</u> One-half (½) of the accumulated income and principal shall be held in trust for the benefit of my son, JACK JOSEPH DOE. The Trustee shall distribute the accumulated income and principal equally over a ten-year period. The Trustee shall also distribute such amounts of income and principal as the Trustee feels my son needs for his health, education, maintenance, and welfare. Except, when Jack reaches the age of forty-five years old, the Trustee shall distribute the remaining accumulated income and principal to my son, JACK JOSEPH DOE. If JACK JOESPH DOE is deceased before he receives his complete distribution, the undistributed income and principal shall be held in trust for the benefit of his children. The Trustee shall distribute such amounts of income and principal for the benefit of the children of JACK as the Trustee feels the children need for their health, education, maintenance, and welfare. The Trustee does not need to make distributions in equal amounts for the benefit of the children of JACK, but shall use his or her discretion to determine how much income or principal each child needs. When the youngest child of my deceased child reaches the age of twenty-five, the Trustee shall then divide and distribute the remaining accumulated income and principal equally between the surviving children of JACK JOSEPH DOE. If JACK is not living and has no surviving children, the remaining accumulated income and principal shall be distributed according to the provisions of Article 5.3(b) for the benefit of his sister.

Jane made certain decisions while she was living about what Jack should receive if John, her husband, was not living. She instructed her successor trustee to divide the trust into two equal parts, one for the benefit of Jack and one for Jamie; distribute Jack's trust equally over a ten-year period; in addition to the $1/10$ distribution annually, evaluate and distribute any additional amount he determines Jack needs for his health, education, maintenance, and welfare; and when Jack reaches age forty-five, distribute all of Jack's remaining trust property to him.

Jane obviously felt that it would be best for Jack to receive distributions equally over a ten-year period. Notice, if Jack is forty-one years old when Jane and John are both gone, Jack will receive $1/10$ of his share of the trust per year for four years, and when he turns forty-five, he will receive the balance of his trust. If Jack is forty-six when Jane and John are both gone, Jack will receive all of his trust immediately, because the triggering event, turning forty-five, has already occurred.

Jane also included a plan if Jack should die before he receives a complete distribution of his trust. If Jack has children, the successor trustee will keep Jack's remaining property in trust for the benefit of Jack's children and use his judgment to determine how much they need for health, education, maintenance, and welfare. The trustee does not have to treat Jack's children equally, but when Jack's youngest child turns twenty-five years old, the trustee must divide the remaining trust account into as many equal shares as Jack has living children and distribute the balance of the trust equally among them. Jack's children do not receive anything from the trust unless Jack dies before receiving his full distributions. Jane also directed the trustee to add Jack's share to Jamie's share if Jack dies without children before the trust is completely distributed.

5.3(b) <u>Trust for the Benefit of My Daughter, JAMIE ANN DOE.</u> One-half (½) of the accumulated income and principal shall be held in trust for the benefit of my daughter, JAMIE ANN DOE. The Trustee shall distribute one-half (½) of the accumulated income and principal when JAMIE ANN DOE reaches the age of thirty (30) years old and the Trustee shall distribute the remainder of the accumulated income and principal to JAMIE ANN DOE when she reaches the age of thirty-five (35) years old. The Trustee shall also distribute such amounts of income and principal as the Trustee feels my daughter needs for her health. However, if Jamie does not graduate from college with a four-year degree by the time she reaches the age of thirty (30) years old, her share shall be forfeited, and shall be paid to her brother's trust according to the terms of Article 5.3(a). If JAMIE ANN DOE is deceased before she receives her complete distribution, the undistributed income and principal shall be held in trust for the benefit of her children. The Trustee shall distribute such amounts of income and principal for the benefit of the children of JAMIE as the Trustee feels the children need for their health, education, maintenance, and welfare. The Trustee does not need to make distributions in equal amounts for the benefit of the children of JAMIE, but shall use his or her discretion to determine how much income or principal each child needs. When the youngest child of my deceased child reaches the age of twenty-five, the Trustee shall then divide and distribute the remaining accumulated income and principal equally between the surviving children of JAMIE ANN DOE. If JAMIE is not living and has no surviving children, the remaining accumulated income and principal shall be distributed according to the provisions of Article 5.3(a) for the benefit of her brother.

Jane made different decisions for Jamie. The successor trustee must divide the trust into two equal parts, one for the benefit of Jack and one for Jamie; distribute ½ of Jamie's trust to her when she turns thirty years old and the remaining ½ when Jamie turns thirty-five (it is irrelevant that the successor trustee is distributing Jack's share equally over ten years); and distribute anything Jamie needs for her health, even if Jamie has not reached the triggering age of thirty or thirty-five. The successor trustee can distribute for Jack's health, education, maintenance, or welfare, whereas the successor trustee can distribute only for Jamie's health. The instructions to the successor trustee about how to distribute Jamie's trust property if she dies before receiving complete distributions are the same as the instructions for Jack's share.

Jamie's trust has a triggering event that is a penalty. If she does not earn a four-year degree by the time she is thirty years old, she forfeits her share of the trust for herself and her children. Maybe this provision was placed in the trust document because Jack already earned his degree, and Jane felt very strongly that Jamie should be motivated.

5.4 <u>Absence of Named Beneficiaries.</u> If there are no beneficiaries named as final distributees living at the termination of this Trust or any Trust created hereunder, then the property remaining in the Trust or Trusts shall be paid and distributed to my heirs at law as though I had died intestate, a resident of Florida.

You should include a provision that tells your successor trustee what to do if all of the beneficiaries you name are gone. In the unlikely event that John, Jack, Jamie, and all of the children of Jack and Jamie are gone, the trust will be distributed as if Jane died intestate. This means the successor trustee will look at the state law in Florida and distribute the trust property to the persons who would have received the property had Jane died without a will. The laws are different in each state about who receives your property when you die without a will. You don't have to have your "absence of named beneficiaries clause" direct a distribution according to the intestate laws of your state. You can instruct your successor trustee to distribute the trust property to other named persons or perhaps to a charity in the event your family is gone.

Assigning a Trustee

When you are naming your successor trustees, you need to ask yourself whether the successor trustee you are considering will be capable, or even alive, to serve. You might want to revisit Chapter 13 about choosing a trustee. This will help you make the right decision.

ARTICLE VI
<u>TRUSTEE</u>

6.1 <u>Trustee While JANE ADAMS DOE Is Living.</u> I hereby appoint myself, JANE ADAMS DOE, as Trustee.

ARTICLE 6.1 names Jane as her own trustee. You will probably name yourself as initial trustee as well.

6.2 <u>Trustee If JANE ADAMS DOE Is Not Living.</u>

6.2(a) <u>Trustee If My Spouse, JOHN ALEXANDER DOE, Is Living.</u> If JANE ADAMS DOE is not living or is not capable of serving, I hereby appoint my husband, JOHN ALEXANDER DOE, to serve as trustee.

ARTICLE 6.2(a) names the successor trustee after Jane is gone or not capable of serving. Jane named her husband, John, as the first successor trustee. If Jane is dead, John will pay all of the debts and any taxes, and then he will distribute the remaining property to his trust.

6.2(b) <u>Trustee If JANE ADAMS DOE and JOHN ALEXANDER DOE Are Not Living.</u> If JANE ADAMS DOE and JOHN ALEXANDER DOE are not living, I hereby appoint ABC BANK to serve as Trustee of any trusts created for the benefit of my children, JACK JOSEPH DOE, JAMIE ANN DOE, or the children of JACK or JAMIE ANN DOE.

ARTICLE 6.2(b) names a successor trustee to serve if both Jane and John are gone or not capable of serving. Jane named a bank as successor trustee when John is gone or not available to serve. She might have chosen a bank because she knew the trust was going to be in place for a long time and didn't want to worry about who would serve as successor trustee for Jack and Jamie, or for their children if either of them died before receiving his or her full trust distribution.

If this were your trust, you might have named Jamie as successor trustee for Jack's trust and Jack as successor trustee for Jamie's trust. You might feel uncomfortable about a bank making decisions for your children or grandchildren. Again, the choices you make depend on what you think is best for your family.

6.3 <u>Fees.</u> The Trustee shall be compensated a reasonable fee for serving as Trustee. The Trustee shall also be reimbursed for all expenses and charges incurred in the performance of its duties or by reason of its office as Trustee.

6.4 <u>Disabled Trustee.</u> A Trustee is "disabled" (and while disabled shall not serve as Trustee) if the next successor trustee receives written certification that the examined trustee is physically or mentally incapable of managing the affairs of the trust, whether or not there is an adjudication of the trustee's incompetence.

6.4(a) <u>Certification of Disability.</u> This certification shall be valid only if it is signed by at least two (2) physicians, each of whom has personally examined the trustee and at least one (1) of whom is board-certified in the specialty most closely associated with the alleged disability. This certification need not indicate any cause for the trustee's disability. A certification of disability shall be rescinded when a serving trustee receives a certification that the former trustee is capable of managing the trust's affairs. This certification, too, shall be valid only if it is signed by at least two (2) physicians, each of whom has personally examined the trustee and at least one (1) of whom is board-certified in the specialty most closely associated with the former disability.

6.4(b) <u>Reliance on Certification.</u> No person is liable to anyone for actions taken in reliance on the certification under this paragraph, or for dealing with a Trustee other than the one removed for disability based on these certifications.

ARTICLE 6.4 puts a plan in the document in the event that any trustee becomes incapacitated. This is an important provision, because without a way to certify a trustee's disability, if Jane became disabled, John would have to have Jane declared judicially incompetent in order to serve as successor trustee. This is a very expensive and cumbersome process that can be avoided by including a process in the trust document to have a trustee removed in the event that he or she becomes disabled and unable to serve.

Miscellaneous Trust Provisions

The remainder of a trust document can be described in a summary manner. The provisions are important to include in your trust document, but do not represent the substance of your plan. Several of the more important miscellaneous trust provisions are described here, but the full text of the remaining trust provisions can be found in Appendix D.

Diversification

You may want your successor trustee to be able to keep the property the trust owned while you were alive even though the trust property might not be the property a reasonably prudent trustee should keep. Therefore, you need to include a clause that does not require the successor trustee to diversify the property owned by the trust after you are gone. See **ARTICLE 7.2** in Appendix D.

Spendthrift and Creditors Clause

You can include a clause in your trust document that prevents your beneficiary from selling or transferring his or her interest after you are gone. It wouldn't do much good to put a detailed plan in place on how the successor trustee should distribute the trust property after you are gone if the beneficiary could sell or transfer his or her interest to get money early. A sample trust provision to accomplish these goals is included at **ARTICLE 7.4** in Appendix D.

The trust can also include a provision that prevents a creditor of your beneficiary from attaching your beneficiary's trust interest before a distribution is made.

Accountings

It is important for your trust document to give your successor trustee instructions regarding how and when the beneficiaries must be provided with accountings. If your successor trustee is not required to give your beneficiaries accountings, the beneficiaries would have no way of knowing what the trustee is doing. If your trustee is not doing his job, your beneficiaries can take the accountings and file a lawsuit to have him removed. A full text of a typical accounting provision is included in **ARTICLE VIII** found in Appendix D.

Signature, Witnesses, and a Notary

You should sign your trust document in the presence of two witnesses and a notary. Some states do not require you to sign in the presence of two witnesses and other states don't require a notary. However, your trust is an important legal document. Don't risk that your trust will be found invalid because it lacked a witness or your signature was not notarized.

Chapter 15

E The Lowdown on Life Insurance

W hile life insurance traditionally pays a death benefit so that your family has enough money to pay the bills, it has also become an investment and a retirement vehicle. This chapter will sensitize you to the types of products available and teach you the rules on how life insurance should be owned and paid to maximize the value of the insurance for your family.

Three Parties to a Policy

In order to evaluate how your life insurance policy should be owned and paid, it is important for you to understand the legal relationship of the parties to a life insurance policy. There are three parties to a life insurance policy: the insured, the owner of the policy, and the beneficiary of the policy.

The insured is you. When you die, the policy pays a death benefit. The owner of the policy is the one who makes all of the decisions about the policy. For instance, the owner can change the beneficiary or make elections about how the policy proceeds will be paid to the beneficiary, and owns all of the insurance policy benefits, such as the cash value, if there is any. Then there is the beneficiary. This is the person or entity that the owner of the policy names to receive the death benefits. Unless you have done some sophisticated planning, you are usually both the owner and the insured of your life insurance policies.

Types of Life Insurance

There are two types of life insurance: term insurance and life insurance policies that have cash values. There are hundreds, maybe thousands, of different varieties of insurance policies within these two types.

Term Insurance

Term insurance is life insurance that has no benefit associated with the policy other than a death benefit. You pay a premium for the term, usually one year, and if you die while the term insurance is in effect, the insurance company pays a death benefit to the person or persons you named as your beneficiaries. If you don't die while the term insurance is in effect, you have nothing left at the end of the term other than the peace of mind of knowing that if you had died, a death benefit would have been paid to your beneficiary.

Life Insurance with Cash Value

A life insurance policy with cash value has two components. It has a death benefit and cash value. In the old days, the insurance company guaranteed a minimum rate of return on the cash component of the policy. If you decided to terminate the policy, you could withdraw at least the guaranteed cash value. If the insurance company earned more than it expected, your cash value could be larger. The variety of insurance products that have a cash value component has increased dramatically.

The insurance companies have become very creative with the options you have regarding the cash value component. For instance, the cash value of some policies is being invested and the growth is being used to pay future premiums. Other policies are using the growth on the cash value to provide a larger death benefit. The goal of yet another type of policy is to maximize the investment yield on the cash value by investing the cash value in mutual funds that own stock to create a larger cash value for you to withdraw.

There is more emphasis on the cash value of life insurance products than there was in the good old days. You should shop around. Contact several agents. You will be surprised to learn how many different products are available.

Depending on your age and your health, the newer life insurance products may provide you with more benefits for the same money. You should contact your life insurance agent and find out if you would be better off converting your existing policy to one that gives you more bang for your buck.

Life Insurance and the Probate Process

Life insurance proceeds can avoid probate if you have selected the right beneficiary. If your life insurance policy is payable to a person and is not paid to your estate, the life insurance death benefit will not be subject to probate. This means that as soon as the named beneficiary files a claim with the insurance company, and the claim is approved, the insurance company will make a direct payment to the named beneficiary. If you have more than one beneficiary, the insurance company will pay the death benefit to the beneficiaries in the proportion you designated when you applied for and purchased the insurance or according to any changes of beneficiary you made since then.

ALERT!

When you are organizing the information about your property, you should locate your life insurance policies. Contact the insurance companies and ask them to send you a copy of your beneficiary election. You may be surprised to recall who you named as a beneficiary or beneficiaries when you purchased the policy.

Payable to the Estate

If you name your estate as the beneficiary of your life insurance, the death benefit will be paid to the executor of your estate when you die and become subject to probate. You might name your estate as the beneficiary of your life insurance if you aren't sure whom you want to name. However, you usually buy life insurance because you want to make sure the person you name as the beneficiary has enough money when you are gone. Therefore it is unusual not to know whom you want to name as the beneficiary.

Then again, some people name their estate as the beneficiary because they didn't realize it would make any difference. You might think that naming your estate as beneficiary is the same as naming a person because you know that your estate will belong to your family. Your life insurance proceeds may end up going to your family, but when you name the estate you are unnecessarily subjecting the insurance death benefits to the cost and delay associated with probate.

Circumstances to Consider

There are other circumstances where you might have named your estate as beneficiary. You will probably want to check up on this if either of the circumstances applies to you.

It is not uncommon that when you are employed, your employer provides employee benefits. One of the benefits that might be offered to you is what is called *group life insurance*. Group life insurance is typically term insurance. It is in force only as long as your employer pays the premiums and you are employed. There is rarely a cash value associated with it. Group life insurance does not mean that a death benefit is paid to a group of people; it means that because you are a member of the employer's group, you are entitled to a stated amount of insurance benefits paid to the beneficiary or beneficiaries you name.

If you have group life insurance through your employment, you should ask the administrator to provide you with a copy of any beneficiary elections you made. If you have named your estate, you might consider changing the election to a person or persons.

When you are filling out all of the paperwork before you start your job, you may not have given much thought to who you wanted to name as the beneficiary of the group life insurance benefit. You may have checked the box on the paperwork that said "pay the death benefit to my estate." In the back of your mind you might have thought that it didn't matter if the beneficiary was a person or your estate; the death benefit would ultimately go to your heirs. However, as you've learned, it does make a difference. By naming your estate as beneficiary, the death benefits will be subject to probate.

Another circumstance that you might not even think about is if you have divorced since you named the beneficiary of your life insurance. You may have named your former spouse as the beneficiary on that policy and did not change this when you finalized the divorce. If so, most state laws treat the former spouse as if he or she were dead, and the policy proceeds will be paid to your estate.

Tax Consequences

A misconception many people have regarding life insurance is that you do not owe taxes on the death benefits. Like many misconceptions, there is some truth to this statement.

Income Tax

Most of the time, your beneficiary will not have to report a death benefit on his or her income tax return. The beneficiary you name does not owe income taxes on the death benefit because the law contains an exemption for death benefits received from a life insurance policy, regardless of whether the beneficiary is a person or estate. There are some exceptions to this rule that probably do not apply to your policies. But if an exception does apply, your beneficiaries will have to report the death benefit on his or her income tax return and pay taxes.

An exception to the exemption from income taxes is if you transferred the policy for value while you were alive. This doesn't happen very often. You are usually both the owner of the policy and the insured person. However, if you became the owner of the policy because you bought the policy from someone else, your beneficiary will lose the income tax exemption. The most common example of a transfer for value is when you are in partnership or are the shareholder of a company. The partnership or company owned the policy and was making the premium payments. If you and your business partners decide to dissolve your business relationship, it would be common that you might buy the policy on your life from the partnership or company. This is a transfer for value.

It is not a transfer for value when you purchase life insurance on your own life from an insurance company because you are the initial owner of the policy. It is rare to have a transfer for value that would make the life insurance proceeds taxable to your beneficiary.

Let's take a look at another example. Someone has insurance on his life and cannot afford to continue to pay the premiums, so you buy the policy from him. While this makes you the new owner, the other person is still the insured. After you buy the insurance, you would probably name yourself or your family as the new beneficiary. This is a transfer for value.

Death Taxes

The fact that life insurance death benefits are not subject to *income* taxes is what leads most people to conclude that there are no taxes owing on these benefits at all. This is not always true.

Most people are both the insured and owner on their life insurance policies. When you die, the insurance proceeds are paid to the beneficiary or beneficiaries you name in the policy. Even though the death benefit is paid to a beneficiary, it is added to your other property that is subject to federal death taxes. Don't panic yet. Read Chapter 18 and calculate your federal death tax. If you discover that your life insurance is causing your estate to owe federal death taxes, it's not too late. It is absolutely unnecessary for your family to pay federal death taxes on the life insurance death benefits they receive. You can create an irrevocable life insurance trust, and in most cases, your family can completely avoid federal death taxes on the life insurance.

FACT

When your estate owes federal death taxes, the starting federal death tax rate is 41 percent and increases quickly to 50 percent. This makes income taxes look cheap. If your estate is subject to federal death taxes, you should strongly consider forming an irrevocable life insurance trust or engage in other planning to remove the life insurance from your taxable estate.

The Irrevocable Life Insurance Trust

Your family would be so disappointed to learn that 41 to 50 percent of the life insurance proceeds they receive when you die must be paid over to the federal government in federal death taxes. This would truly make the government your heir and not your family. You can avoid the federal death taxes by forming an irrevocable life insurance trust.

Before you study irrevocable life insurance trusts, you should read Chapter 18 and calculate whether your estate will owe federal death taxes. You can have $1,000,000 of taxable base before your estate will owe taxes. The death benefit on a life insurance policy that was owned by you is included in your taxable base and may push your estate over the $1,000,000 limit. You may think that there is no way you have $1,000,000. However, when you read Chapter 18 you will discover that certain items are included in your taxable base, such as the life insurance death benefits, that you did not expect to be subject to federal death taxes.

It Pays to Do Your Homework

If you need an irrevocable life insurance trust, you are going to need professional assistance to establish the trust. The mechanical aspects of creating an irrevocable insurance trust and filing the forms that may be required with the IRS are beyond the scope of this book. However, you can learn what an irrevocable trust does and be prepared with the information your lawyer will need to create the document for you. This will substantially reduce the cost of creating it.

The first thing you should do is read Chapters 11, 12, and 13. Those chapters teach you all about trusts. In many ways, an irrevocable insurance trust is like the trusts you have already learned about. You will need to decide who will be trustee and make the same decisions about how your beneficiaries will be paid after you are gone as you would make if you were creating a revocable trust that becomes irrevocable after you die. While these aspects are familiar to you, there are some exceptions and differences you need to be aware of.

There are three major differences with an irrevocable life insurance trust. First, the trust is irrevocable. Second, you should not serve as the trustee of the irrevocable life insurance trust. Third, there may be a gift tax consequence for transferring your life insurance policy to the trustee of the irrevocable insurance trust.

Transferring Ownership

After you create your irrevocable insurance trust, you will transfer ownership of your life insurance policy to the trustee. You will still be the insured on the life insurance policy, but you will no longer be the owner. When ownership is changed, the beneficiary of the policy will be changed from whomever you had previously named to the trustee of your irrevocable insurance trust. In other words, your irrevocable life insurance trust will be both the owner of your insurance policy and the beneficiary.

Interpolated Reserve Value

If the insurance policy has an interpolated reserve value, you are making a gift of the interpolated reserve value to the beneficiaries of your irrevocable insurance trust. The interpolated reserve value is a value that is very close to the cash value of your insurance policy. You should contact your insurance agent and ask him or her how much the interpolated reserve value is for your policy.

Calculating the amount of the gift and filing the necessary gift tax return when you transfer a life insurance policy to an irrevocable insurance trust is not something even most lawyers can do. You need the help of a lawyer who specializes in this area of the law and establishes irrevocable trusts on a regular basis. The lawyer who helps you calculate any gift involved with transferring your policy will also explain to you how the premiums should be paid after the trust is created, and how those premium payments might affect a federal death tax owing when you die.

Most of the time a lawyer spends to create an irrevocable trust involves teaching you about trusts and the choices you need to make for your beneficiaries. You can save a lot of money by being prepared.

Getting Help

You are now ready to make an appointment with a lawyer. Explain to the lawyer that you know about irrevocable insurance trusts, have decided who will serve as trustee, have determined the powers you would like the trustee to have, and have ascertained the interpolated reserve value of the policy. The lawyer will be impressed that you even know how to say the words interpolated reserve value, not to mention the fact that you already have that information.

If you have a $100,000 life insurance policy that would have triggered a $41,000 federal death tax bill, it is more than worth your money to create an irrevocable insurance trust.

If you are equipped with this information, it should not take a lawyer who works in this area much longer than three or four hours to meet with you and prepare the irrevocable trust document. If your meeting with the lawyer leads to other issues, he or she will charge an hourly rate to do other work for you.

A Simpler Solution for Life Insurance

There is an easier way to remove your life insurance from your taxable base: You can gift the policy to your beneficiary. By doing this, you will still be the insured person, but now your beneficiary will be both the owner and the beneficiary. If your beneficiary also owns your life insurance policy, the policy proceeds payable at your death will not be subject to federal death taxes.

Beware, however, if you make your beneficiaries the owner of your life insurance policy, you have given them all the rights you had, including the right to withdraw the cash value from the policy. Although it is simpler to gift your life insurance policy directly to your beneficiaries, you do not have the control you would have if you transferred ownership of your policy to an irrevocable trust. Also, when you create an irrevocable insurance trust, you have named a trustee who must follow the instructions you put in the document. These instructions can protect both the current cash value of your policy and put a plan in place on how the death benefit will be managed and distributed after you are gone.

ALERT!

Remember, you need only be concerned about your life insurance if your taxable base, as described in Chapter 18, is more than $1,000,000. When the cost of making a mistake is paying the federal government 41 cents on the dollar, it's time to get some help.

If you decide to take the simple path and gift your insurance policy to your beneficiaries, you will still need the assistance of a professional to help you compute the gift you might be making because of your policy's interpolated reserve value. (E)

Chapter 16

E All about Annuities

Annuities have become very popular investment vehicles. Typically, annuities are sold by insurance companies, financial institutions, and brokers. There are as many varieties of annuities as there are makes and models of cars. Before you decide if one is right for you, you need to understand how annuities operate and how they are taxed.

What Is an Annuity?

An annuity is a contract or agreement between you and the company selling the annuity, the issuing company. You give the issuing company a certain amount of money, and in turn it promises to invest your money and repay you according to the option or payment method that you choose. Of course, it isn't as simple as that, so let's get to the legal basics.

There are three parties in an annuity contract: the owner of the annuity, the annuitant, and the beneficiary. (You can have multiple beneficiaries to an annuity.) Annuities have some of the attributes of life insurance and some characteristics of an individual retirement account.

The owner is the person or entity that owns the annuity. You are typically the owner of your annuity. But you can create an entity, like a trust, to own your annuity. The owner has the right to choose the beneficiaries, the right to withdraw money from the annuity, and the power to make decisions about how the annuity is invested.

The second party to the annuity contract is the annuitant. The annuitant is often the same person as the owner of the annuity and may be the one who will be receiving the annuity payouts. The annuitant's life expectancy is used to calculate payment options, and when he or she dies, the annuity is paid to the beneficiary or beneficiaries chosen by the owner of the annuity. The age of the annuitant will have a significant effect on how the withdrawals from the annuity are taxed.

There are hundreds, maybe even thousands, of elections you can make about how the issuing company invests your annuity money. When you purchase an annuity, the salesperson, bank, broker, or financial advisor will provide you with information about how your annuity can be invested.

The beneficiary is the third person involved with an annuity. The beneficiary is the person or entity that the owner of the annuity names to receive the annuity payments. Typically you will name yourself as the first, or primary, beneficiary of the annuity contract, and you will name another person or entity, called a successor beneficiary, to receive the annuity payments after you are gone.

Investment Choices

The choices you have regarding how your annuity is invested are very similar to the investment choices you could make if you did not invest in an annuity. The issuing company can place your money in very secure funds, like treasury or bond funds, or it can invest your annuity in aggressive growth funds. Like any other investment, the risk of losing money increases when you choose more aggressive investments for your annuity.

Issuing companies have developed numerous options, guarantees, and inducements to persuade you to buy their annuity product. It would be impossible to describe all of these financial inducements. Some issuing companies provide a life insurance feature, others promise a higher rate of return for a period of time, and some provide a minimum rate of return. These are examples of typical financial "add-ons" to induce you to purchase that particular annuity contract.

When you meet with your salesperson, broker, or bank, you need to ask the salesperson to explain very carefully each feature of the annuity you are thinking about buying. It is difficult to compare one annuity with another, because the issuing companies have given many of their annuity features cute little names. It is very important for you to shop around to make sure you are getting the best product for the money.

Annuities and the Probate Process

The only way an annuity can be subject to probate is if you name your estate as the beneficiary or if the beneficiaries you name are dead. If your beneficiaries are all dead, the annuity will automatically be paid to your estate.

When you buy an annuity contract you should not name your estate as the beneficiary. One of the advantages of an annuity is that the issuing company will pay the annuity directly to your named beneficiary or beneficiaries after you are gone. When the annuity is paid directly to a named beneficiary, the annuity will avoid probate.

ALERT!

While avoiding probate is a big incentive to purchase an annuity, be sure you know all the facts before contacting an issuing company. Annuities have disadvantages that may outweigh the advantage of avoiding probate.

Income Tax Consequences

Annuities are taxed differently than other investments. Some advisors think annuities are the best thing since sliced bread. Other advisors will tell you that annuities are the worst investment you could possibly buy. It's up to you to figure out if annuities will meet the needs of your family. Understanding the rules will help you make this decision.

Special Treatment

Annuities are granted special income tax treatment. But you need to be very careful; the tax advantage you enjoy while you are living becomes a disadvantage to the person or persons you name as beneficiaries once you are gone.

FACT

The amount you earn is greater with an annuity than a taxable investment because you are not paying income taxes on the annual growth of the annuity. But keep reading—there is a payback.

An annuity is like an individual retirement account. While you are living, the earnings from the annuity will not be subject to income taxes. You pay income taxes on the earnings only when you withdraw or receive payments from the annuity contract. The ability to defer the income taxes owing on the annual earnings is a very important feature of an annuity.

For example, when an annuity earns 5 percent in a one-year period, there are no income taxes paid on the earnings that year. The income taxes will be paid when you withdraw from your annuity. Compare this tax-deferred return with 5 percent you might earn from your savings account. Earnings from your savings account are subject to income taxes, even if you don't withdraw the money during the year. Therefore, if your savings account earns 5 percent, and 20 percent is your marginal income tax bracket, you really only earned 4 percent after-tax, because you must pay 1 percent in income taxes (20% x 5% = 1%).

Penalty for Early Withdrawal

Annuities were granted this special income tax deferral to encourage you to save for your retirement. To try to ensure that you use annuities for retirement planning, there is a penalty if you withdraw money from your annuity before you reach age 59½. Unless you meet one of the exceptions, if you withdraw money from your annuity before you reach age 59½, you will be charged an additional 10 percent income tax on the earnings.

For example, if you are in the 20 percent marginal tax bracket, and you withdraw $1,000 of earnings from your annuity before reaching age 59½, you will pay $300 in income taxes on the withdrawal rather than $200. Your normal marginal rate was 20 percent, but the additional 10 percent income tax charged means you pay a 30 percent tax on the annuity earnings you withdraw.

ALERT!

The income tax deferral of an annuity is a double-edged sword. As long as you don't touch the money in the annuity contract, it grows tax-free. When you withdraw money from your annuity, you pay income taxes on the portion of the withdrawal that represents earnings.

The main exception to paying the additional income tax is if you withdraw the money from the annuity equally over the rest of your life. For example, assume your annuity is worth $100,000 and you are forty years old. At age forty, your life expectancy is 42½ more years. (Your life expectancy is established by IRS tables.) If you want to avoid the additional 10 percent income tax, you can withdraw only 2.3529 percent of the annuity each year. The 2.3529 percent is computed by dividing 1 by 42.5 (2.3529% x $100,000 = $2,352.94). As you can see, the exception doesn't help you much if you need more money now than the fractional amount payable over the rest of your life.

Annuities Affect Cost Basis

The reason some advisors think annuities are the worst investment you can buy is because of what happens after you die. To understand this, you need to learn the rules about cost basis. When you buy a piece of property, the amount you pay for the property is your cost basis. For example, if you buy one share of ABC stock for $50, $50 is your cost basis in the stock. If you buy a house for $125,000, $125,000 is your cost basis in the house.

QUESTION?

Why do people buy annuities knowing that the growth will not get a new cost basis when they die?
When you buy an annuity, the salesperson stresses the fact that the annuity will grow yearly and you will not pay annual income taxes. But very few salespeople explain to you that when you die, your beneficiaries will pay all of the income taxes you didn't pay while you were alive.

When you die, the person who receives your property (we will call this person your heir) gets a new cost basis equal to the value of your property on the date of your death. If the one share of ABC stock you bought for $50 is worth $80 when you die, your heir gets a new cost basis in that stock equal to $80. Now, if your heir sells the one share of stock for $80, she has no gain on the sale. When you sell a piece of property, your gain is computed by taking the selling price, in this case $80, and subtracting the cost basis, which is also $80 in this case ($80 − $80 = $0).

The rules are different for annuities. Annuities do not receive a new cost basis when you die! This is a tremendous disadvantage for your beneficiaries.

Assume you bought an annuity for $50,000 when you were forty years old, and you don't withdraw any money. You are now sixty-five years old. If your annuity earned 6 percent (tax-free) for twenty-five years, it would be worth $214,593. Now assume you die at age sixty-five. Your beneficiary takes your cost basis of $50,000. She does not get a new cost basis. If your beneficiary withdraws all of the money from the annuity in one year after your death, she will owe about $46,000 in income taxes!

If you had bought almost any other type of property for $50,000, and you died when that asset was worth $214,593, your heirs would receive that property with a new cost basis equal to $214,593, the value of the property on the date of your death. If your heirs sold the property they would have no income tax. The selling price would be $214,593 minus their new cost basis of $214,593, equaling $0 gain.

Death Tax Consequences

The full value of any annuity you own is included in your federal death tax base. It is irrelevant that the annuity is paid directly to your beneficiary. The annuity is included in your federal death tax base because you *owned* the annuity. If you did not own the annuity, it would not be included. (Chapter 18 teaches you how to calculate your federal death tax exposure.)

If you already own annuities, it is important that you do two things. First, calculate whether your estate is subject to federal death taxes. If so, you need to realize that the federal death taxes begin at a 41 percent marginal rate. This means that if you own a $100,000 annuity, your beneficiary could pay $41,000 in federal death taxes. If you determine that your estate is not subject to federal death taxes, you don't have to worry about your annuity creating a federal death tax.

Second, contact the issuing company where you bought the annuity or the agent from whom you bought the annuity. Ask the issuing company or agent to send you your cost basis in the annuity and what the annuity is currently worth. If you have been taking withdrawals from your annuity, it is almost impossible for you to compute your cost basis. When you receive the information, subtract the cost basis from the value of the annuity. This is the amount of income your beneficiary will have to report as income after you are gone. Remember, your beneficiary does not get a new cost basis equal to the value of the annuity as he or she would if this were any other type of asset.

Let's say you bought an annuity for $50,000 and it is worth $455,026 when you die. If your estate is subject to federal death taxes, your family could pay up to $202,513 in death taxes attributable to the annuity! Don't worry, Chapter 19 shows you how to reduce federal death taxes.

Annuities as Part of Your Plan

If you had a crystal ball and knew when you were going to die, owning an annuity could be a good choice for you. Unfortunately, we simply cannot see into the future. To evaluate how an annuity fits into your plan, you should:

- Follow the instructions in Chapter 18 and compute your federal death tax exposure.
- Determine which pieces of property will not get a new cost basis when you die.
- Calculate the income taxes your beneficiaries will owe on the pieces of property that do not get a new cost basis.
- If your estate will owe taxes, read Chapter 19.
- Make an appointment with a good tax lawyer if you don't like what you see.

Making Use of Your Annuity

By planning ahead, you can make the best use of your annuity. For instance, let's say you are sixty-five years old and think you're going to live until you're eighty. You have an annuity that is worth $455,026 and decide that you want to use annuity withdrawals for your support rather than selling other assets to produce income. If you begin withdrawing approximately $46,850 per year from your annuity when you are sixty-five years old, and the annuity continues to earn 6 percent per year, your annuity will be spent by the time you are eighty.

If you combine a $46,850 withdrawal from your annuity with your social security, this may be a comfortable amount for you to live on. With the deductions and exemptions you have on your annual income tax return, the tax you owe may be far less than the income taxes that would be owed by your beneficiaries if you did not make withdrawals from your annuity.

When you examine the other pieces of property you own—each neatly described on a separate piece of paper—you may discover that if you spend money from your annuity, you are letting other assets grow. Those other assets will get a new cost basis when you die, and your heirs will owe no income taxes on those other assets.

There is only one problem with this plan. Unfortunately—or maybe fortunately—you don't know if you are going to live until you are eighty years old. There's no way to know when you are going to die. If you have organized all of the information about your property, it will be much easier to have your tax attorney, your financial planner, or your banker run projections for you to show you how you might spend money while you are alive to save your family money after you are gone.

FACT

Analyzing whether an annuity should be part of your plan is complex. However, when you understand the income and estate tax rules about annuities, you can make the best decision for your family.

Advantages and Disadvantages

There are advantages and disadvantages to owning annuities. The advantages are that an annuity will be paid to your beneficiary and will not be subject to probate. The earnings from an annuity contract are tax deferred until you make a withdrawal. When you don't pay annual income taxes on the earnings, the annuity will grow more quickly. The disadvantages are that your beneficiaries do not get a new cost basis in the annuity when you die and will owe the income taxes you did not pay. Also, your annuity is included in your federal death tax base, and is therefore subject to federal death taxes.

These are advantages and disadvantages you should consider before you buy an annuity. If you already own one or more annuities, you should figure out how the annuity fits into your plan while you are living, and how owning the annuity will affect your beneficiaries after you are gone.

Chapter 17

Reviewing Retirement Accounts

If you are considering a retirement plan or already have one, it is important to know what happens to your retirement account when you are gone and how it will be taxed when you make withdrawals. The information in this chapter will be mostly limited to IRAs. However, you will be alerted when the rules also apply to employer-provided retirement plans.

Retirement Accounts and the Probate Process

All retirement accounts are alike, whether they are IRAs or employer-provided plans, as far as whether they will be subject to probate. Retirement accounts are like annuities: The only way a retirement account can be subject to probate is if you named your estate as the beneficiary or if the beneficiaries you named are dead.

If your employer established a retirement account for you, the administrator of the retirement account gave you an application to complete. On that application, you named one or more beneficiaries to whom your retirement benefits would be paid after you are gone. You may have completed that paperwork years ago. It is important that you contact the plan administrator and ask for a copy of your beneficiary election. If you want the retirement benefits to avoid probate, you need to make sure that you did not name your estate as the beneficiary.

The rule is the same for IRAs. The only way your IRA will be subject to probate is if you name your estate as the beneficiary. You may have multiple IRA accounts. You should contact the administrator of all of your IRA accounts and request a copy of your beneficiary election form.

ALERT!

If you are gone and your home is sold and your address has changed, your family may never find your retirement accounts unless you keep the information together in an organizational system.

Who receives your retirement benefits is governed entirely by your beneficiary election. Unless you have named your estate as the beneficiary, whatever you put in your will or trust will be completely disregarded.

Obtaining a copy of your beneficiary election forms serves two purposes. First, you can confirm that you did not choose your estate as the beneficiary. Second, when you have organized your paperwork in a notebook or in some other manner, your family will know where to find information about your retirement accounts after you are gone.

Naming Your Beneficiary

In the old days choosing a beneficiary of your retirement accounts was a simple matter. The husband named the wife as beneficiary and the wife named the husband as beneficiary. The children were typically named as successor beneficiaries who received the retirement benefits if both spouses were gone. This was the typical pattern because it met the needs of the traditional family. It would be fair to say that there are more families today that are nontraditional.

Because divorces and remarriages are common today, choosing a beneficiary of your retirement plan may require balancing the security you want to provide your second spouse with the needs of your children from a former marriage. For instance, you may decide to name your children from a former marriage as beneficiaries of your retirement plan and provide for your current spouse with your other property. In order to decide what is best for your family, you need to understand the rules about naming your spouse as the beneficiary of your retirement plan versus naming someone else, such as your children.

The law about when you can change your beneficiary elections for your IRA accounts changed dramatically in January 2001. The new law allows you to change your beneficiary elections at any time. Prior to 2001, once you turned age 70½ you had to make all of your elections about your IRAs, including naming your beneficiary, and those elections became irrevocable. Now you can change your beneficiary even if you are older than 70½.

Naming Your Spouse as Beneficiary

When you name your spouse as the beneficiary of your IRA, your spouse has two options: He can either transfer the balance of your IRA into a new IRA or into his existing IRA, or he can assume your IRA.

If your spouse either transfers your IRA into a new IRA or into his existing IRA, he will be able to change the successor beneficiaries. This means that if you named your spouse as your primary beneficiary and you named your children from a former marriage as your successor beneficiaries to receive the IRA after your spouse is gone, your spouse can change the successor beneficiaries you chose. Your children from a former marriage may discover after the death of your spouse that they will not receive the remaining retirement benefits you worked so hard to accumulate.

ALERT!

Don't feel pressured to name your spouse as the beneficiary, especially if you have children from a former marriage. Remember, this is your decision to make. You must feel comfortable and confident with your choice of beneficiary.

The second election your spouse can make is to assume your existing IRA. If this happens, your spouse's age the year after your death will determine how rapidly he or she must withdraw from your IRA. The advantage of having your spouse assume your IRA is that the persons you name as successor beneficiaries will receive the remaining balance after your spouse is gone. The disadvantage is that after the death of your spouse, his age expectancy the year after his death will determine how rapidly the successor beneficiaries must withdraw from the IRA. This will probably create a much more rapid payout of the IRA than it would if the ages of younger beneficiaries, such as your children, were used to calculate the required distributions.

Of course, it is much easier when you have been married to the same person, and any children you may have are your children. Then, you almost always name your spouse as the beneficiary and your children as the successor beneficiaries.

Understanding the elections your spouse has is easier under the new law, but it is still very complex. You may want to consult with a professional to decide the best choice for you and your family.

Naming Non-Spouse Beneficiaries

If you have children and no spouse, you will probably name your children as the beneficiaries of your IRA. Even if you have a spouse, you may still decide to name your children as the primary beneficiaries. This typically happens because this is either a second marriage for you, or you and your spouse have evaluated all of your property and determined that your family unit can save taxes this way.

If you have no spouse or children, you will need to choose someone or some entity as the beneficiary. There are no limits on who you can name. However, your choice of who you name may be affected by how your IRA will be taxed.

If you have a retirement account established by your employer, you need to contact your employer's plan administrator to learn the rules about who you can name as beneficiary and how the retirement account proceeds will be taxed. The rules for employer-sponsored retirement plans can vary, depending on the plan.

Income Tax Consequences

There are many types of retirement accounts that could have been established by your employer. Your employer might have made all of the contributions to the retirement account on your behalf, or you might have made some of the contributions. How withdrawals by you or by your beneficiaries will be taxed depends on when the plan was set up, who made the contributions, and how the contributions were characterized when they were made. It is impossible to make a blanket statement about how the withdrawals from an employer-provided plan will be taxed. You need to contact your plan administrator and ask.

IRAs, on the other hand, are all governed by the same rules. It doesn't matter who is the administrator or bank holding your IRA account. There is one set of rules about how IRA withdrawals are taxed when you make the withdrawal, and there is a second set of rules about how withdrawals will be taxed to your IRA beneficiaries after you are gone.

Usually an employer-provided retirement plan can be transferred to your IRA after you retire. Again, you'll need to contact the plan administrator to determine your options. With the new IRA rules, it will probably provide you with more flexibility to transfer any employer-provided retirement plan into your individual IRA.

Income Taxes When You Withdraw

All withdrawals you make from your IRA must be reported on your income tax return in the year you withdraw the money. There are no special income tax rates available for your withdrawals. However, there is a penalty if you withdraw money from your IRA before you turn age 59½—an additional 10 percent tax on the withdrawal. The 10 percent penalty is calculated in the same way as the 10 percent income tax penalty for annuities as described in Chapter 16.

There are five exceptions to the penalty for taking a distribution before you reach age 59½. You will not have to pay the 10 percent penalty if:

1. The distribution is due to your death.
2. The distribution is made because you are disabled.
3. The distribution is made for certain qualified medical expenses.
4. The distribution is $10,000 or less and is used to purchase your first home.
5. The distribution is for educational expenses following high school.

You must begin taking withdrawals from your IRA in the year you turn 70½. The amount you must withdraw each year is established by an applicable divisor schedule that has been established by the IRS. For instance, when you are seventy-two years old, you must withdraw 4.09836 percent of the total value of your IRA that year. If your IRA is worth $100,000, you must withdraw $4,098.36.

FACT

The rationale for making you take distributions from your IRA when you reach age 70½ is to try to force you to spend all of your IRA before you die. This is why the required minimum distributions are calculated based on your life expectancy.

The percentage you must withdraw each year changes. Contact the financial institution that manages your IRA. They will give you a copy of the schedule and show you how much your required distribution will be each year. Or if you would like more information about how to make the calculations and determine how much you must withdraw each year, check the resources section in Appendix B.

If you are married and your spouse is more than ten years younger than you, you may elect to have your IRA paid over the joint life expectancy of you and your spouse. This will result in a lower or smaller annual distribution. Hopefully, this assures that there are enough IRA benefits that will be paid for the rest of your life and your spouse's life.

Income Taxes for Your Beneficiaries

Withdrawals your beneficiaries make from your IRA after you are gone are taxed in the same manner as withdrawals you might have made while you were alive. Namely, when your beneficiary makes a withdrawal from the IRA, she will report that withdrawal on her income tax return. And if your beneficiary makes an excess withdrawal before she turns 59½, she will also have to pay the 10 percent penalty tax, in addition to her regular tax rate. Of course, if your beneficiary withdraws money for one of the five exceptions, she will not pay the 10 percent penalty tax.

When you die, your IRA can be divided into separate shares for each of your named beneficiaries. The life expectancy of the youngest beneficiary is used to calculate how quickly all of the beneficiaries must take their distributions. (The IRS has published a single life expectancy table to determine how rapidly your beneficiaries must withdraw from the IRA after you are gone.)

The beneficiaries will need to withdraw a stated percentage each year. But because the stated percentage is based on the life expectancy of the youngest beneficiary, the length of time over which the beneficiaries must withdraw is extended dramatically. For instance, if your youngest beneficiary is fifty-four years old when you die, the stated percentage for a fifty-four-year-old person is 3.3898 percent. If your beneficiary's portion of the IRA is $100,000, your beneficiary must withdraw $3,389.83 that year. This amount will change every year. You can obtain a chart on how to compute the required annual distributions for your beneficiaries from the administrator of your IRA. Or you can check the resource section in Appendix B for additional guidance, or to confirm that the withdrawal rules have not changed.

Your beneficiaries will pay income taxes on your IRA after you are gone. The longer the IRA stays in an account, the more opportunity it has to continue to grow tax-deferred for the benefit of your beneficiaries.

Death Tax Consequences

The full value of your IRAs as of the date of your death will be included in your federal death tax base. Chapter 18 teaches you how to calculate your federal death tax exposure. You may have thought that because your IRA avoids probate and is payable directly to a named beneficiary, it is not subject to federal death taxes. Unfortunately, this isn't true.

Chapter 16 provided advice about annuities as part of your plan. The same advice is appropriate for your IRAs. There is one difference. The beneficiaries of your annuities pay income taxes only on the growth or gain on the annuities. With an IRA, your beneficiaries pay income taxes on 100 percent of the IRA distributions they receive after you are gone; therefore, the combined income taxes and death taxes can be even larger for your IRAs than your annuities.

Planning Ahead

You should consider spending your IRAs while you are living, and let your other property grow in value. The other property you own will receive a new cost basis equal to the value of the property when you die, and there are no income taxes owing when your heirs receive your property as there is with an IRA. (Cost basis was explained in detail in Chapter 16. If you have not read Chapter 16, you might want to check there to learn about cost basis.)

FACT

The combined death tax and income taxes on your IRA can top out at 87 percent of the value of your IRA. If your federal death tax rate is 50 percent, and the income tax rate your beneficiaries pay is 37 percent, then 87 percent of the value of your IRA will be paid in taxes.

If you follow the recommendation about how to analyze the property you own, you will be determining whether your estate has a federal death tax exposure, and you will be thinking about whether your beneficiaries or heirs would owe less in income taxes on the property they receive from you if you do the right planning. Remember, you don't have a crystal ball. If you knew when you were going to die and when your spouse was going to die, you would know exactly how much to withdraw from your IRA to minimize the taxes owing. You can only make an educated guess. This is why it is important that you review your plan at least every year to see if it still meets your needs.

Chapter 18
Death and Taxes

You've heard people say that only two things in life are certain: death and taxes. You work your whole life to accumulate property only to discover that when you die the federal government becomes your heir. When you understand the rules about federal death taxes, it is much easier to reduce the federal government's inheritance.

What Is the Federal Death Tax?

The tax your estate might owe when you die will be referred to in this chapter as a *transfer tax* and not a death tax. This is because taxable gifts are added to the transfers you make when you die to determine a taxable base. Then the taxes your estate owes when you die are a percentage of your taxable base, if your taxable base exceeds a certain amount. Confused? Don't worry, read on.

Unified Transfer Tax

The federal death tax is not a stand-alone tax. In 1976 Congress changed how federal death taxes were computed. Taxable gifts you make during life are combined with the taxable transfers you make when you die, and the total transfers are subjected to a "unified transfer tax." Gifts and transfers at death are added together to tax your "unified transfers" to prevent you from escaping taxes at death by giving away your property while you are living.

The easiest way to understand the unified transfer tax is to think of it like a piggy bank. The federal government grants you a piggy bank of a dollar amount. Your piggy bank is technically called an *exemption equivalent*. You can use your piggy bank to make gifts or transfers while you are living, or you can use your piggy bank to shelter transfers you make at death.

Piggy Bank Amount

Congress has changed the piggy bank amount over the last fifteen years. In May 2001 Congress increased the piggy bank from $675,000 per person to $1,000,000 per person. For example, your piggy bank is currently $1,000,000. If you make a taxable gift of $300,000 while you are living, you only have $700,000 of piggy bank left when you die. Right now, the rate is 41 percent for transfers between $1,000,000 and $1,250,000.

To complicate things even further for you and your family, the piggy bank is scheduled to increase until the year 2010, when it will become unlimited. In the year 2010 you can transfer as much property as you want, either during life or at death, and pay no transfer taxes. The piggy bank amount, or exemption equivalent, is scheduled to increase according to the following schedule:

Year	Exemption Equivalent
2004	$1,500,000
2006	$2,000,000
2009	$3,500,000
2010	Unlimited

Unfortunately, you can't count on the increase. With a stroke of a pen, the scheduled increase can be repealed. You can only plan on the exemption equivalent in effect now—$1,000,000.

ALERT!

Congress frequently changes the tax rules when they figure out that the tax breaks they provided cost the government too much in lost revenue. So don't plan your death assuming that effective 2010 there will be no transfer taxes!

Property That Is Subject to Federal Death Taxes

The property that is taxed when you die, along with the taxable gifts you made while living, is referred to as your *taxable base*. Almost everyone understands that property you own when you die might be subject to federal death taxes or transfer taxes. What most people don't understand is that the taxable base is much broader than merely property you own when you die. When you finish reading this chapter you may find yourself adding pieces of paper to your notebook to describe property you never dreamed would be taxed.

Property You Own When You Die

The first category of property included in your taxable base is all of the property you own in your individual name. You may have organized this information in your notebook or when you completed the estate-planning worksheet found in Appendix C. If you own property in joint name with your spouse or someone else, do not include that property on your list yet. Keep reading: There is a section in this chapter that will teach you how to calculate the amount of property that must be included in your taxable base attributable to joint property. The first step to computing your taxable base is to add up the value of all of the property that is titled in your individual name.

Life Insurance

The amount of life insurance proceeds that will be paid to anyone when you die is the second category of property subject to transfer taxes when you die. You probably don't consider life insurance as property you own. As a matter of fact, you may have thought that because your life insurance is paid directly to the beneficiary named in the policy, there are no taxes. While life insurance benefits are not subject to income taxes, the proceeds are included in the calculation of your taxable base.

You should return to your notebook and prepare a separate piece of paper for each life insurance policy you have. Before you list the necessary information about your life insurance policies, you may want to read Chapter 15. Chapter 15 teaches you the difference between the owner, the insured, and the beneficiary of the life insurance policy. Chapter 15 also shows you how you can remove the life insurance proceeds from your taxable base.

Imagine how shocked your family would be if they found out that the $500,000 life insurance policy you paid for all of your life pushes your taxable base over your $1,000,000 piggy bank amount, and they owe $210,000 in transfer taxes when you die, just on your life insurance!

Annuities

When you prepared your pieces of paper describing each piece of property you own, you should have also completed one piece of paper for each annuity you own. Chapter 16 teaches you about how annuities are taxed and how you might plan now to minimize those taxes.

The value of any annuities received by anyone because of your death is included in your taxable base. This may confuse you. You were probably told that one of the terrific things about annuities is that they grow in value tax-free. This is not even a half-truth; it's probably closer to a one-quarter truth. While you did not pay income taxes on the growth of you annuity while you were alive, when you die, the value of the annuity on the date of your death is included in your taxable base. If your taxable base exceeds the piggy bank amount of $1,000,000, a minimum of 41 percent of the annuity will be paid in transfer taxes.

ALERT!

The income taxes you deferred and did not pay will be paid by the beneficiaries of your annuity after you are gone. The combined income taxes and transfer taxes when you die can easily exceed 70 percent of the value of the annuity.

Retirement Accounts

You may have the same misconception about retirement accounts as you do about annuities. You may think that because your retirement accounts are paid directly to a named beneficiary, they are not subject to transfer taxes at death. This is simply not true. The full value of most retirement accounts is included in your taxable base. There are some special rules for certain employer-provided retirement accounts, so you should always check the rules with your plan administrator. In order for you to calculate your transfer tax exposure when you die, you need to add up the value of all of your retirement accounts.

FACT

Please keep in mind that in addition to transfer taxes that might be owing because of your death, the beneficiaries of your retirement accounts will also pay income taxes on distributions after you are gone. Chapter 17 gives you valuable tips on how you can structure your retirement account beneficiary elections to reduce income taxes.

Joint Property

A portion or all of your joint property is included in your taxable base even though the property passes automatically to the surviving joint tenant. The amount that is included in your taxable base is different if the joint tenant is your spouse, as opposed to a joint tenant who is not your spouse. If your joint tenant is your spouse, you include 50 percent of the value of the joint property in your taxable base. It does not matter which spouse paid for the property.

If you own property with a joint tenant who is not your spouse, the percentage you contributed toward the purchase price of the property will be included in your taxable base. For instance, if you paid for 100 percent of the cost of the joint property, then 100 percent of the value of the joint property will be included in your taxable base. If you paid for 80 percent of the cost, and the other joint tenant paid for 20 percent, then you include 80 percent of the value of the property in your taxable base.

Property in Your Power

If you make any transfer of property while you are living and you keep the power to alter, amend, or revoke the transfer, the full value of the property you transferred will be included in your taxable base—the value of the property at the date of your death, not the value the property had when you made the transfer.

The most common example of property you might transfer over that you hold a power to revoke is a revocable trust. The property in the revocable trust will avoid probate, but because you hold a power to revoke the trust, the value of the trust assets will be included in your taxable base.

If you transfer property but are still using or enjoying the property when you die, it is still included in your federal taxable base. This is a tricky one for the person who tries to do his or her own planning. The classic example is when you deed a piece of property to someone else. For instance, you deed your home to your child. Your child owns the property, but you continue to live in the home, rent-free. Because you enjoyed the use of the property until you died and did not pay rent, the value of the property is included in your taxable base.

General Powers of Appointment

If you hold a general power of appointment over property, the full value of that property will be included in your federal taxable base. If you think you hold a general power of appointment over property, you might want to read about powers of attorney in Chapter 20.

It is a tedious process to calculate your federal death tax exposure. But this is what your family is going to have to do after you are gone. It is so much better if you are alive to help your family with this calculation, rather than leaving them to find the information they need after you are gone, and then perhaps being surprised by the result when it is too late to plan.

Taxable Gifts

Because you need to add taxable gifts you made during your life to your taxable base when you die, you need to understand the definition of a taxable gift. It would be unrealistic to expect you to keep records of every single gift you make. Therefore the law defines a taxable gift as a gift above a certain amount per year made to any person. The amount you can give each year is called the *gift tax exclusion.*

ESSENTIAL

Because the annual exclusion is available to as many persons as you would like to gift to, you can reduce your taxable base substantially by engaging in annual gifting at an amount less than the annual exclusion to each person. Annual gifting is a core building block in many estate plans. You may want to include this in your estate plan as well.

For many years the gift tax exclusion was $10,000 per year per person. It is important to understand that the gift tax exclusion is a per person exclusion. If you have four children and six grandchildren, you could give $100,000 per year, or $10,000 to each person, without making a taxable gift that would affect your piggy bank.

To make your life more complicated, as part of the tax reform passed by Congress, the annual gift tax exclusion amount will be increased periodically to account for inflation. The current gift tax exclusion is $11,000 for the year 2003. Every person can give the gift tax exclusion amount to as many people as he or she wants. Therefore, if you are married, you and your spouse can each give $11,000 without making a taxable gift.

How to compute transfer taxes at your death changed for transfers after December 31, 1976. Prior to that time there was a gift tax for taxable gifts you made and a different death tax for transfers you made at death. Both taxes have been unified. Now, *one* tax is paid on the taxable gifts you make during your life and the transfers you make at death. The total of all taxable gifts you have made since December 31, 1976, are added back to your taxable base. There are adjustment rules for gifts made before December 31, 1976, which are beyond the scope of this book.

Deductions Against Your Taxable Base

The information you gathered in your notebook will help you determine the deductions you can take against your taxable base. There are four categories of items that can be deducted against your taxable base:

1. Funeral and administration expenses, claims against your estate, unpaid bills, and debts and taxes
2. Casualty and theft losses
3. Charitable gifts you make at your death
4. Most property you leave to your spouse

Debts and Funeral Expenses

If you prepared the notebook described in Chapter 2, you have already listed the debt owing against each piece of property you own. Or, if you completed the estate-planning questionnaire (see Appendix C), you listed and summarized the debts you owe. All debts you owe at the time of your death are deductible against your taxable base.

Funeral expenses and the cost of administering your estate after you are gone are also deductible against your taxable base. If you have done your homework, the cost of administering your estate will be substantially less than it would have been. Without planning, the average cost of administering an estate after a person is gone is 1 percent times the value of all assets owned by the person who died.

Charitable Gifts

Any contributions to a qualified charity are deductible from your taxable base. If your estate contributes cash to a charity, the amount of cash you contribute will be deductible from your taxable base. If your estate contributes property to a charity, the value of the property contributed is deducted from your taxable base.

FACT

You usually don't need to worry about whether a charity is qualified. Churches, schools, hospitals, and most national and state associations that benefit a purpose are qualified charities. The reason there are limitations on donating to a nonqualified charity is that the government does not want you to try to transfer property to your family, friends, and neighbors and characterize the transfer as a charity.

Property Left to Your Spouse

When you compute your taxable base, you are allowed to subtract the value of all property transferred to your surviving spouse, as long as you are leaving your spouse a qualified interest. This is called the *marital deduction*. If you leave property to your spouse with no strings attached, this is a qualified interest. No strings attached means your spouse can do whatever she or he wants with the property after you are gone. Chapter 19 covers the restrictions you can place on a transfer to your spouse and still qualify for the marital deduction. Before you learn what types of restrictions you can place on a transfer to your spouse at death, you need to fully understand why you may or may not want a marital deduction.

A marital deduction operates like this: If you die with a $500,000 taxable base, and you leave all of your property to your spouse, you will subtract the $500,000 transfer to your spouse, and your taxable base is now zero. Remember, your taxable base includes all of the items described in this chapter. When your taxable base is zero, your estate is not using any of your piggy bank, or exemption equivalent. Now, when your spouse dies, she has all of the property that would have been included in her taxable base, plus the $500,000 she received from you.

Should You Leave All of Your Property to Your Spouse?

The answer depends on the total value of the marital taxable base. The marital taxable base is the sum of the husband's taxable base and the wife's taxable base. The exemption equivalent has been referred to for simplicity purposes as the piggy bank amount—$1,000,000. The $1,000,000 piggy bank is a "use it or lose it" benefit. If you do not use your piggy bank when you die, you can't give your piggy bank amount to your spouse.

For instance, assume the husband has a taxable base of $800,000. Assume the wife has a taxable base of $300,000. If the husband leaves all of his property to the wife, his estate will have a zero taxable base because his estate subtracts the $800,000 left to his wife. The husband did not use any of his piggy bank because his taxable base was zero. Now his wife dies. Her taxable base is $1,100,000 ($800,000 received from her husband plus her $300,000 taxable base). The tax owing on the death of the wife is $41,000.

ALERT!

You want to be careful that you do not overfund your surviving spouse. Your surviving spouse has only one piggy bank of $1,000,000. If you leave your spouse too much property, your surviving spouse might have a larger taxable base than he or she has in available piggy bank.

If the husband had left $700,000 to his wife outright, and $100,000 of property in a way that his wife could have the benefit of the property but did not own it outright, and then his wife died, her taxable base would be $1,000,000 ($700,000 received from her husband and her own $300,000 taxable base). She would have a $1,000,000 piggy bank to offset any transfer taxes owing at her death, and the family would owe no taxes on the death of the wife. (Chapter 19 will teach you how the extra $100,000 can be owned for the benefit of the surviving spouse, not be included in the surviving spouse's taxable base.)

If you and your spouse's combined taxable bases exceed $1,000,000, as in the preceding example, you should consider not leaving all of your property to your spouse. However, if the combined taxable base of both spouses is under $1,000,000, there is no adverse death tax consequence to leaving all of your property to your spouse.

Figuring Your Federal Death Taxes

It's time to figure out whether or not you will owe federal death taxes (or transfer taxes), and if so, how much you will owe. Are you ready? First take out your notebook and add up all property that is taxed when you die, along with the taxable gifts you made while living. This gives you your taxable base. Next add up all deductions you might take as described in this chapter. Then subtract the deductions from the taxable base. This number will determine if or how much you will owe in transfer taxes.

If your taxable base is **less than $1,000,000** there are no transfer taxes at death.

If your taxable base is **over $1,000,000** your estate will owe the following transfer taxes:

Taxable base of $1,000,000–$1,250,000:
The transfer tax will be 41 percent times the amount over $1,000,000.

Taxable base of $1,250,000–$1,500,000:
The transfer tax will be $102,500 plus 43 percent of the amount over $1,250,000.

Taxable base of $1,500,000–$2,000,000:

The transfer tax will be $210,000 plus 45 percent of the amount over $1,500,000.

Taxable base of $2,000,000–2,500,000:

The transfer tax will be $435,000 plus 47 percent of the amount over $2,000,000.

Taxable base of $2,500,000–$3,000,000:

The transfer tax will be $670,000 plus 49 percent of the amount over $2,500,000.

Taxable base over $3,000,000:

The transfer tax will be $915,000 plus 50 percent of the amount over $3,000,000.

(These rates will change at the top end from 2003–2010.)

If your taxable base, after all other deductions, is more than your piggy bank amount, move on to Chapter 19. Several methods to reduce the transfer taxes are covered, including charitable giving and charitable trusts. If any of the tax-planning suggestions described in Chapter 19 appeals to you, more homework should be done before you make your final decision on how to reduce the transfer taxes when you die. Developing a plan to pay no transfer taxes, commonly known as death taxes, is a game. There are many ways to win! Ⓔ

Chapter 19

(E) How to Reduce Taxes

I t is very gratifying to create an estate plan that reduces or eliminates taxes. The federal death tax is very expensive. If your family owes federal transfer taxes, the beginning rate is 41 percent! You will discover that with some planning, most families can substantially reduce or eliminate this tax.

Credit Shelter Trusts

Credit shelter trusts are used only between spouses, when needed. The credit shelter trust is really a slang term; there is no legal definition. It has become known as a credit shelter trust because of how it uses the unified transfer tax credit.

When the federal death taxes, or transfer taxes, are computed on your estate, your estate is actually granted a tax credit equal to the piggy bank, or exemption equivalent, amount. When you create a credit shelter trust, you are creating a trust that uses the tax credit associated with the piggy bank amount. That is why it is called a credit shelter trust. Don't panic; as you continue reading, you will understand these concepts.

ALERT!

If you add your taxable base to the taxable base of your spouse, and the total exceeds one piggy bank amount, you should definitely consider using credit shelter trusts.

A credit shelter trust is really not a separate trust. It is created within a revocable trust. While you are alive, you are your own trustee and have full control over the trust property. But when you die, the successor trustee takes over and begins following the instructions you put in your trust document. The credit shelter trust becomes alive when you die if the combined taxable base of you and your spouse exceed one piggy bank amount.

If your taxable base plus the taxable base of your spouse is less than one piggy bank amount ($1,000,000), your successor trustee will probably be instructed to transfer the entire balance of your trust to your spouse's trust or to your spouse outright since you don't need a credit shelter trust to reduce your death taxes. It is only when your surviving spouse would have a taxable base larger than $1,000,000 that you use a credit shelter trust for death tax planning.

When you die, your revocable trust becomes irrevocable. If you have created a credit shelter trust, there will be instructions in the trust document that will tell your successor trustee to look at your surviving spouse's potential taxable base. There are two possible sets of instructions that could be given, depending on the combined taxable base of you and your spouse.

Perhaps there are other reasons why you don't want your spouse to have access to your property. In which case, you may instruct your successor trustee to keep your property in trust to be managed for the benefit of your spouse or your other beneficiaries after you are gone. But this is not creating a credit shelter trust to reduce taxes.

The First Set of Instructions

The first set of instructions would cover the situation where the combined taxable base of your estate plus your spouse's estate is between $1,000,000 and $2,000,000. If this occurs, the first thing your successor trustee will do is calculate what your surviving spouse's taxable base would be if he died. Remember, your spouse might receive property because of your death from sources other than your trust. If your spouse received insurance proceeds, annuities, or retirement accounts because of your death, those amounts should be included in his taxable base. The successor trustee will then be instructed to transfer enough property from your trust to your surviving spouse or his revocable trust to leave him with a taxable base equal to the piggy bank amount.

FACT

If the combined taxable base of you and your spouse is $1,500,000, as illustrated in the following example, your family saves $210,000 in death taxes that would be owing on the death of the second spouse merely by creating a credit shelter trust inside of your revocable trust.

For example, assume your surviving spouse has a $700,000 taxable base. This taxable base already includes insurance, annuities, or retirement plans your spouse received because of your death. Assume your taxable base is $800,000. If the piggy bank or exemption equivalent is $1,000,000, your trustee would transfer $300,000 of your trust property to your spouse's trust. This would leave your spouse with a taxable base of $1,000,000. Then, if your spouse dies, there will be no death taxes, because your spouse has a $1,000,000 piggy bank to shelter his or her taxable base. If your successor trustee transferred $300,000 from your trust to your spouse's trust, there would be $500,000 left in your credit shelter trust.

The Second Set of Instructions

The second set of instructions tells your successor trustee what to do if the combined taxable base of you and your spouse is over $2,000,000. If your combined taxable bases are over $2,000,000, when you die, your successor trustee will be instructed to transfer all of your trust property over $1,000,000 to your spouse's trust.

For example, assume your taxable base is $1,200,000 and your spouse's taxable base is $1,100,000. Your successor trustee would keep $1,000,000 in your credit shelter trust and transfer $200,000 to your spouse or his revocable trust. The $200,000 is deducted from your taxable base because you can deduct property you give to your spouse. This would leave you with a taxable base of $1,300,000. Your estate would pay no taxes because the taxable base equals the piggy bank exemption equivalent.

If your surviving spouse is left with a taxable base of more than $1,000,000, hopefully he will be able to do some planning to reduce his taxable base below $1,000,000. These examples assume that neither you or your spouse made any taxable gifts during your lives that would reduce the available piggy bank or exemption equivalent when you die.

ALERT!

You cannot name your spouse as successor trustee of your credit shelter trust. If you do, the credit shelter trust will be included in your spouse's taxable base when she dies, and you will have wasted your time creating it. Your spouse does not have full control over the credit shelter trust property, but if you choose a friendly trustee, it is close.

Power over the Trust Property

In the first example, you had $500,000 in the credit shelter trust. In the second example, there is $1,000,000, the maximum piggy bank amount, in the credit shelter trust. The credit shelter trust is irrevocable after you are gone. Your successor trustee will manage the money or property in it for the benefit of your family according to the instructions you put in the document.

You can give your trustee any of the powers that are described in Chapters 11 and 12 over the trust property. If you recall, you can be very specific about how, when, and why your successor trustee distributes the credit shelter trust money and property for your spouse, your children, or other beneficiaries you might name. But frankly, what most people want is to provide their surviving spouse with as much access to the property in the credit shelter trust as possible. However, there are rules about how much access you can give to the property without causing the credit shelter trust to be included in your spouse's taxable base when he or she dies.

FACT

If the combined taxable base of you and your spouse is over $2,000,000, you have saved your family $345,800 in federal death taxes by creating credit shelter trusts inside of your revocable trust.

You can give your spouse the absolute right to all of the income from the property. In addition, you can give your trustee the power to distribute as much money or property from the credit shelter trust as your spouse needs for her or his health, education, maintenance, or welfare. And you can give your surviving spouse the right to demand the greater of $5,000 per year or 5 percent of the value of all of the credit shelter trust assets. This power to demand is in addition to the other rights and powers.

Make Gifts of Your Assets

Gifting property to your family while you are living is an excellent estate-planning device. It is simple and does not involve expensive legal fees to accomplish. You can reduce the size of your taxable estate very quickly by making gifts that are not taxable and do not consume your piggy bank.

Limit on Gifting

Careful planning with the use of your annual exclusions can be an extremely effective wealth-transfer device. You are allowed to give $11,000 per year to as many people as you would like to include in your annual gifting plan. This amount will increase periodically to reflect inflation. As long as you do not gift more than $11,000 per year to any one person, your gifts will not consume your piggy bank or exemption equivalent.

If you have ten family members to whom you are comfortable making annual gifts, you can reduce your taxable base by $110,000 per year. If you are married, your spouse can either make gifts from his individual property or join with you in a gift you are making to give $22,000 to each person. If you and your spouse make annual gifts to ten people, you can reduce your taxable bases by $220,000.

Gifting Property

You do not have to give cash to use the annual exclusion. You can give property. And you don't have to give all of one piece of property away in one year. For example, assume you have four children, and you own a piece of property that is worth $200,000. You and your spouse could give 44 percent of the property to your children this year, 44 percent next year, and the remaining 12 percent of the property in the third year. You can do this without using any of your piggy bank because you and your spouse gifted each child $22,000 per year for the first two years and $6,000 in the third year.

If you exceed the annual exclusion amount for any person during the year, you begin to consume your piggy bank. If you own property that you think is going to increase in value very rapidly, it might make sense to use up your piggy bank with taxable gifts. If you give away a $1,000,000 piece of property, using all of your piggy bank, and the property becomes worth $3,000,000 by the time you are gone, the $2,000,000 of growth is not in your estate. If your estate is in the 50 percent tax bracket, you save $1,000,000 of transfer or death taxes by using your piggy bank while you are living.

The richest of the rich use annual gifting to decrease their taxable estates. When you analyze the property you own, the cost basis of each piece of property, and your family's exposure to federal death taxes, you will be able to decide if you want to make gifts to reduce your taxable base.

Qualified Personal Residence Trust

Many of the more sophisticated estate tax reduction tools use the concept of giving away property now at a discounted value. A qualified personal residence trust is one of those sophisticated estate tax reduction techniques. A qualified personal residence trust is referred to as a *QPRT*. A QPRT is a way to transfer your personal residence to the next generation at a fraction of the transfer tax cost. The amount of savings your family will enjoy will depend on two factors: the length of time for which you establish your QPRT and your age when you create the QPRT.

Understanding QPRT

The best way for you to understand a QPRT is to imagine that the title to your home is represented by a piece of paper. If you take that piece of paper and cut it into two pieces, you have divided the title to the property into two pieces. This is really what you do when you create a QPRT. You cut the title to your property into two pieces. One piece represents the use of your home for a specified number of years, called the term of years. The second piece of the paper represents the title to your home after the term of years, called the remainder interest.

When you create a QPRT you decide how long or how many years you want the term of years to last. You will keep the first piece of the title for that number of years, meaning you continue to live in your home the way you did before you created the QPRT. Then you gift the other piece of the paper, representing the remainder interest in your home, to someone else, typically your children. After the end of the term of years your children own your home.

ALERT!

If your family is exposed to federal death taxes it is very important that you review your plan annually. If your property is not properly titled or you don't manage how much property is in the name of each spouse, your family could pay unnecessary taxes.

Time Value of Money

A QPRT is designed around the time value of money. The best way to understand this concept is to consider the value of $1 in the future. The right to have $1 today is not equal to the right to receive $1 five years from now; the value of $1 five years from now is worth less than the value of $1 today. The difference in value depends on the interest rates. If interest rates are 5 percent, the value of $1 five years from now is 78 cents. If interest rates are 11 percent, the value of $1 five years from now is 58 cents. The higher the interest rates, the lower the present value of a dollar payable in the future.

FACT

If you create a QPRT for ten years when the interest rates are 5 percent, the present value of the right to have your $100,000 home ten years from now is $61,000. That is because the present value of the right to receive $1 ten years from now is 61 cents on the dollar.

Let's say you own a home worth $100,000, and you create a QPRT for five years when interest rates are 5 percent. You are giving away title to your home now with possession delayed for five years. It is exactly like giving away the right to have $1 five years from now. This means that you can transfer your home to your children, or whomever you name as your beneficiary, at a transfer tax value of approximately $78,000 rather than $100,000. The time value of money makes what you give now worth 78 cents on the dollar. (It is impossible to make a blank statement about how the gift will be affected by you age.)

Saving Money in Your Piggy Bank

By creating the five-year QPRT you have given away a home worth $100,000 for $78,000. The reason this is significant is because taxable gifts you make during your life consume your piggy bank amount. If you make a taxable gift of $100,000 when the exemption equivalent is $1,000,000, you have $900,000 of exemption equivalent left to use against the transfers you make when you die. If you make a taxable gift of $78,000 because you created a QPRT to discount the value of the gift, you have $922,000 of exemption equivalent left to use against your death transfers. When interest rates are higher, you get even more benefit from the time value of money when you create a QPRT. The game is to give property to your family at the lowest possible value in order to consume the least amount of your exemption equivalent.

There's a Catch

There is a trick to the QPRT. In order to have the QPRT respected when you die, you have to outlive the number of years you choose for your QPRT. For example, if you create a five-year QPRT and die anytime during the five-year period, it's like you didn't do anything. The house will be included in your estate and the gift you made when you created the QPRT will be ignored. It is important if you are going to create a QPRT to pick a number of years that you realistically think you will outlive. The further you go into the future, the more tax advantage you gain from creating a QPRT, but you have to live the specified number of years.

Adjustment to the Value

You have been shown the calculations as if there is only one factor involved in valuing the gift when you create a QPRT. However, there is also an adjustment to the value based on the probability that you will not live for the number of years you have projected. This part of the calculation is very complex. It is only important for you to know that the gift you make to your beneficiary will be even less if you establish the QPRT when you are older. This is because there is an increased chance that you will die during the QPRT period, which would nullify the gift you made.

FACT

Federal death taxes begin at a rate of 41 percent and are due on the full value of an asset included in your estate. The income rate due on the sale of your home is usually 20 percent calculated only on the gain. If your home is subject to federal death taxes, your family will save more by creating a QPRT.

Disadvantages to a QPRT

The recipient of the property at the end of the QPRT period does not receive a new cost basis. The recipient takes a lower cost basis in the home. Remember the chapters on annuities and IRAs? If the cost basis in your home is significantly less than the value of the home, the savings in death taxes your family gets by creating the QPRT will be reduced by the amount of income taxes your family will pay if they sell the house after you are gone.

Your family could avoid the income taxes on the sale of your home if the recipient of the property at the end of the QPRT period moves into the home and occupies the home as her principal residence. Then, if she occupies the home as her principal residence for two out of the five years before the sale, she could exclude $250,000 of gain if she is a single person, and $500,000 of gain if she is married.

You suffer the main disadvantage associated with a QPRT. At the end of the QPRT period you have to either move out of your house or rent it back from the recipients of the QPRT. You don't own your home anymore. If you stay in the home, you must pay rent. And the rent needs to be the same amount of rent a stranger would pay if he or she rented the home. Paying rent can be a good thing because it is another way for you to reduce the size of your taxable estate.

A QPRT is sophisticated estate-planning device that is typically used by wealthy families as part of their estate plan to reduce taxes. Wealthy families usually use a combination of tax-saving devices. But a QPRT is not just for rich people. It is a technique available for any family that needs to reduce their federal death tax bill.

Grantor Retained Annuity Trusts

A grantor retained annuity trust, referred to as a GRAT, is another sophisticated tax-planning device that allows you to make a gift at a discounted value. The theory of a GRAT is very similar to a QPRT.

A GRAT is a trust where you transfer property into the name of a trustee who holds and administers that property for your benefit and then, after a stated number of years, conveys the property to the persons you designate as your beneficiaries. The number of years you choose for a GRAT will affect the amount of discount you receive on the transfer. The amount of discount you receive from a GRAT is identical to the amount of discount you receive when you create a QPRT. If you create a five-year GRAT with $100,000 of property when the interest rates are 5 percent, you have given away $100,000 of property for a taxable transfer (or gift value) of approximately $78,000. There will be an adjustment due to your age.

ESSENTIAL

> Tax planning is not just for rich people. It is about understanding the rules and knowing how to pick the tools that meet the needs of your family. It is about making estate planning a part of your yearly checkup.

The GRAT is also like a QPRT because you must live for at least the number of years for which you establish your GRAT. If you create a GRAT for five years, and you die after four years, the property in the GRAT trust will be included in your estate. Therefore, there is also an adjustment to the amount of gift to account for the probability that you will not live longer than the number of years for which you created the GRAT.

If you own property that you think will appreciate in value very rapidly and might push your estate over the piggy bank or exemption equivalent amount, a GRAT is an excellent estate-planning tool. However, it is not a device that you can create without the help of a qualified lawyer. The calculations involved in computing the value of the gift and filing the necessary gift tax returns necessitate that you seek the advice of a very competent professional. But knowing how a GRAT operates will help you decide whether this is an appropriate part of your estate plan.

Chapter 20
Power of Attorney

A power of attorney is a legal document that gives someone else, referred to as the holder of the power of attorney, the right to do something for you. Powers of attorney are used to give the holder the power to make legal or financial decisions for you and sign the necessary papers to accomplish the task.

Types of Power of Attorney

Your power of attorney can be very broad or it can be very narrow. A broad power of attorney allows the holder of the power of attorney to do or sign almost any documents you could have signed. A limited power of attorney, on the other hand, allows the holder of the power of attorney to do only the specific acts you include in the document. You can give the holder of your power of attorney the power to use his or her powers at any time, or you can create a triggering event that allows the holder of your power of attorney to exercise his or her powers.

QUESTION?

What is the difference between power of appointment and power of attorney?
Power of appointment is a right given to a specified person within a will or trust to distribute your property. Power of attorney is a legal document granting a specified person the right to act on your behalf.

Broad Power of Attorney

The typical powers in a very broad power of attorney are:

- Power to do any act, thing, or personal or business transaction that you can do
- Power to sue in your name and collect money owed to you from any source
- Power to establish any financial accounts in your name
- Power to terminate any financial accounts in your name
- Power to buy or sell any type of property owned in your name
- Power to improve, maintain, rent, or lease any of your property
- Power to sign any contract in your name
- Power to sign your name to any tax returns

There are only a few things you cannot give the holder of a power of attorney the authority to do on your behalf. Typically you cannot grant someone the power to fulfill a contract that requires your personal services. For example, if you are the quarterback for your local NFL team, you cannot give someone else the power to throw the football at next Sunday's game. You can't grant a power for someone else to complete a legal affidavit that requires your personal knowledge. You can't give someone the power to vote in an election for you. And you cannot give someone else the power to make a will for you.

Limited Power of Attorney

By creating a limited power of attorney, you can either limit what the person who holds a power of attorney can do or specify a triggering event that must happen before the holder of the power can use his or her power. It is very common to give someone a limited power of attorney to get something done for you when you are not available. For example, you can give someone the power of attorney to buy or sell property in your name. The described property could be a car, a house, or a boat. You name it, and you can give someone the power of attorney to buy or sell that piece of property on your behalf. Alternatively, your power of attorney might include a triggering event that must happen before the power of attorney is valid. The most common triggering event is if you become disabled or incapacitated.

ESSENTIAL

Your family may never need to have a power of attorney because hopefully, you will never be incapacitated. But when tragedy strikes, your family has so many issues to deal with, it is an act of love for you to be prepared.

Reasons for Having a Power of Attorney

You should have a power of attorney that gives the holder of the power of attorney the authority to sign at least necessary documents in the event that you become disabled or incapacitated. Most young people don't think about what would happen if they become incapacitated because it seems so unlikely that it will happen. Many older persons don't like to admit that incapacity is a probability; therefore, they ignore what might happen. The bottom line is, if you are incapacitated, no one can sign your name on anything that is in your individual name without a power of attorney.

Consider the following example. You and your wife are both forty years old. You are driving down the street when your car is hit head-on. You are unconscious and transported to the hospital, where you remain in a coma for several months. It is expected that you are going to recover; it's just going to take time. Luckily, your employer provided disability insurance benefits. But the insurance company must issue the benefit check in your name. If your wife does not have a power of attorney, she can't sign your name. Further assume that the savings account where you keep most of your money is also in your name. Again, your wife can't withdraw money. Her only recourse is to file a petition in court to have you declared incompetent, so that she can access the savings account and your disability checks.

ESSENTIAL

You may want to review your documentation to determine what property is titled in your individual name. If your family would need to access any of that property in the event that you become incapacitated, you need a power of attorney.

You might think that if your property is in joint name with your spouse you don't need a power of attorney. Consider the example about the car accident. If both you and your spouse were incapacitated, there would be no one who could access any of your funds. If you have minor children, someone would have to petition the court to have a guardian named. If your money is not available, it makes it very difficult to pay a lawyer to help.

Sample Power of Attorney

A power of attorney is very easy to prepare and can be such an important document for your family. The following is a sample power of attorney. As you will see, this is a very broad power of attorney. When creating your own, you will decide what powers to give to the holder of the power of attorney.

DURABLE POWER OF ATTORNEY

KNOW ALL MEN BY THESE PRESENTS, that I am hereby creating a Durable Power of Attorney.

That I [insert your name], of [insert city], [insert state], do hereby appoint [name the person you would like to appoint] as my attorney-in-fact for me and in my name, place and stead, and for my use and benefit to exercise all of the powers enumerated below, should I be incapacitated. If [person you named] is not reasonably available or is unable to act, then I appoint [name a successor person] as substitute or successor attorney-in-fact to serve with the same powers, in the event I am incapacitated.

I. POWERS

SECTION 1: To exercise, do, or perform any act, right, power, duty, or obligation whatsoever that I may have or may acquire the legal right, power, capacity to exercise, do, or perform in connection with, arising out of, or relating to any personal item, thing, transaction, business, business property, personal property, or real property (including my homestead), or matter whatsoever.

SECTION 2: To ask, demand, sue for, collect, and hold all sums of money, debts, bonds, notes, checks, drafts, accounts, legacies, interest, dividends, stock certificates, certificates of deposit, annuities, pension retirement benefits, insurance benefits and proceeds, and documents of title as I now have or shall hereafter become due, owing, payable, owned, or belonging to me or in which I have or may acquire any interest.

SECTION 3: To establish, utilize, and terminate accounts (including margin accounts) with security brokers; to establish, utilize, and terminate managing agency accounts with corporate fiduciaries.

SECTION 4: To establish accounts of all kinds, including checking and savings, for me with financial institutions of any kind, including but not limited to banks and thrift institutions, to modify, terminate, make deposits to and write checks on or make withdrawals from and grant security interests in all accounts in my name or with respect to which I am an authorized signatory (except accounts held by me in a fiduciary capacity), whether or not any such account was established by me or for me by my attorney-in-fact, to negotiate, endorse, or transfer any checks or other instruments with respect to any such accounts; to contract for any services rendered by any bank or financial institution.

SECTION 5: To purchase, lease, invest, exchange, assign, and acquire, and to bargain, contract, sell, agree to lease, purchase, and exchange, and take, receive, and possess any real or personal property, intangible or mixed, wherever located, including without being limited to commodities, contracts of all kinds, securities of all kinds, bonds, debentures, notes (secured or unsecured), stocks of corporations, regardless of class, interest in limited partnerships, real estate or any interest in real estate, including but not limited to my homestead, whether or not productive at the time of investment, interest in trusts, investment trusts, whether of the open and/or closed funds types, and participation in common, collective, or pooled trust funds or annuity contracts, without being limited by any statute or rule of law concerning investments by fiduciaries, whatsoever upon such terms and conditions as my said attorney-in-fact shall deem proper and to execute any leases, deeds, conveyances, bills of sale, or other instruments of conveyance in connection with either the purchase or sale of any said property, real or personal; to make gifts to my family but not to exceed $10,000.00 to any one person per year, and to any charitable organization described in Section 170(c) and 2522(a) of the Internal Revenue Code of 1986.

SECTION 6: To improve, repair, maintain, manage, insure, rent, lease, sell, release, convey, mortgage, and hypothecate and in any way and manner deal with all or any part of any personal or real property (including my homestead), business, business property, or any other property, which I now own or may hereafter acquire.

SECTION 7: To sign, endorse, execute, acknowledge and deliver, receive and possess such contracts, agreements, options, deeds, conveyances, mortgages, security agreements, bills of sale, leases, insurance policies, documents of title, checks, drafts, certificates of deposit, notes, satisfactions of mortgages, and such other instruments in writing of whatever kind and nature as may be necessary or proper to the exercise of the rights and powers herein granted.

SECTION 8: To prepare, execute, and file any income, gift, or other tax return or claim, federal, state, or municipal, or agency thereof, specifically including Federal Income Tax Return Form 1040 for the years 1989 through 2025, for which I am responsible or to which my property is subject, and to do all things reasonably necessary with respect thereto; to pay any taxes, duties, or assessments, and collect any claims arising therefrom; to negotiate with the appropriate tax authorities, and to litigate or compromise any differences that may arise, with respect to any tax obligations.

SECTION 9: To create a Qualified Income Trust within the meaning of the Medicaid Act, or rules promulgated thereunder, and/or the Omnibus Budget Reconciliation Act as they now exist or may hereafter be amended.

SECTION 10: I grant to my said attorney-in-fact full power and authority to do and perform all and every act and thing whatsoever requisite, necessary, and proper to be done and exercise any of the rights and powers herein granted, as fully to all intents and purposes as I might or could do if personally present.

II. LIMITATION OF POWERS

Notwithstanding the powers contained in this Durable Power of Attorney, my attorney-in-fact may not:

1. Perform duties under a contract that requires the exercise of my personal services;

2. Make any affidavit as to my personal knowledge;

3. Vote in any public election on my behalf;

4. Execute or revoke any Will or Codicil on my behalf;

5. Create, amend, modify or revoke any documents or other disposition effective at my death or transfer assets to an existing trust created by me unless expressly authorized by this Power of Attorney; or

6. Exercise powers and authority granted to me as trustee or as a court-appointed fiduciary.

III. STANDARD OF CARE

Except as otherwise provided herein, any attorney-in-fact named herein is a fiduciary who must observe the standards of care applicable to trustees. My attorney-in-fact is not liable to third parties for any act pursuant to this Durable Power of Attorney if the act was authorized at the time. If the exercise of power is improper, my attorney-in-fact is liable to interested persons for damage or loss resulting from a breach of fiduciary duty by my attorney-in-fact to the same extent as the trustee of an express trust. If my attorney-in-fact has accepted appointment either expressly in writing or by acting under this Power, my attorney-in-fact is not excused from liability for failure either to participate in the administration of assets subject to this Power or for failure to attempt to prevent a breach of fiduciary obligations hereunder.

IV. STANDARD OF CARE LIMITATION

My attorney-in-fact shall not be liable for any acts or decisions made by him in good faith and under the terms of this Durable Power of Attorney.

V. THIRD PARTY RELIANCE

1. Any third party may rely upon the authority granted in my Durable Power of Attorney until the third party has received notice as provided herein.

2. Until a third party has received notice of revocation pursuant to the terms contained herein, partial or complete termination of this Durable Power of Attorney by adjudication of incapacity, suspension by initiation of proceedings to determine incapacity, my death, or the occurrence of an event referenced in this Durable Power of Attorney, the third party may act in reliance upon the authority granted in this Durable Power of Attorney.

3. A third party that has not received written notice hereunder may, but need not, require that my attorney-in-fact execute an affidavit stating that there has been no revocation, partial or complete termination, or suspension of this Durable Power of Attorney at the time the Power of Attorney is exercised. A written affidavit executed by my attorney-in-fact under this paragraph may, but need not, be in the form prescribed by F.S. §709.08, as amended.

4. Third parties who act in reliance upon the authority granted to my attorney-in-fact hereunder and in accordance with the instructions of the attorney-in-fact will be held harmless by me from any loss suffered or liability incurred as a result of actions taken prior to receipt of written notice of revocation, suspension, notice of a petition to determine incapacity, partial or complete termination, or my death. A person who acts in good faith upon any representation, direction, decision, or act of my attorney-in-fact is not liable to me or to my estate, beneficiaries, or joint owners for those acts.

VI. NOTICE

1. A notice, including, but not limited to, a notice of revocation, partial or complete termination, suspension, or otherwise, is not effective until written notice is served upon my attorney-in-fact or any third party relying upon this Durable Power of Attorney.

2. Notice must be in writing and served on the person or entity to be bound by such notice.

VII. DAMAGES AND COSTS

If any third party unreasonably refuses to allow my attorney-in-fact to act pursuant to this Durable Power of Attorney or challenges the proper exercise of authority of my attorney-in-fact, the prevailing party in any judicial action under the applicable section will be entitled to damages, including reasonable attorney's fees.

VIII. REVOCATION OF PRIOR INSTRUMENTS

By this instrument I hereby revoke any power of attorney, durable or otherwise, that I may have executed prior to the date of this Durable Power of Attorney.

I hereby confirm all acts of my attorney-in-fact pursuant to this Power.

Any act that is done under this Power between the revocation of this instrument and notice of that revocation to my attorney-in-fact shall be valid unless the person claiming the benefit of the act had notice of the revocation.

IX. VALIDITY AND DURATION

This Durable Power of Attorney shall not be affected by my subsequent incapacity and shall be exercisable from the date in which I have executed this Power of Attorney, notwithstanding my later disability or incapacity. All acts done by my attorney-in-fact pursuant to the powers conferred herein during any period of my disability or incapacity shall have the same effect, and inure to the benefit of and bind the principal or his or her heirs, devisees, and personal representatives as if the principal were competent and not disabled. The powers, rights, and duties conferred by this Power of Attorney upon my attorney-in-fact shall begin on the date set forth below and shall continue until my death or until it shall be revoked by me in writing.

This Durable Power of Attorney shall be nondelegable, except as to the authority to execute stock powers or similar documents on my behalf and delegate to a transfer agent or similar person the authority to register any stocks, bonds, or other securities either into or out of mine or a nominee's name, and shall be valid until such time as I shall die, revoke the Power, or shall be adjudged totally or partially incapacitated by a court of competent jurisdiction.

I may revoke this Power only by providing written notice to my attorney-in-fact. All acts of my attorney-in-fact taken or done without actual knowledge of (1) my death or (2) my revocation, are valid and effective, and are hereby ratified and confirmed.

This instrument has been executed in multiple counterpart originals. All such counterpart originals shall have equal force and effect.

IN WITNESS WHEREOF, I have set my hand and seal this _____ date.

Signed, sealed, and delivered in the presence of:

_____   _____
Witness Number One   YOUR NAME

_____
Witness Number Two

STATE OF
COUNTY OF

I HEREBY CERTIFY that on this day before me, an officer duly qualified to take acknowledgments, personally appeared **YOUR NAME**, who is (Notary choose one) [_____] personally known to me, or [_____] who has produced _____ as identification, and to me known to be the person described in and who executed the foregoing instrument and acknowledged before me that he executed the same.

WITNESS my hand and official seal in the state and county aforesaid this [insert date].

_____

Notary Public
My Commission Expires: _____

Decisions to Make

The decisions you need to make depend on how much power you are going to give to the person who will hold a power of attorney for you. The more powers you are going to give, the more careful you need to be about the selection of the person you will name.

Review the powers described in the sample power of attorney. This sample is a very broad power of attorney. However, you can go through and strike any power you don't want the holder to have. For instance, you may not want anyone to be able to borrow against your property. Or you may not want the holder to be able to sell your property. But remember, if you eliminate the power to sell, the holder of your power of attorney can't sell anything, even if you need the proceeds to pay bills.

Once you have carefully reviewed the list of powers, it will help you decide who should hold your power of attorney. You should name a person to act as the primary holder of your power of attorney and you should also name a substitute or successor who can serve if the first person you named is not available.

The decisions you need to make to create a power of attorney are:

1. What powers are you going to give?
2. When can the holder exercise his or her powers?
3. Whom do you want to name?

Naming More Than One Person

Naming more than one person is often a way to increase your comfort level. You may feel that you want two people to approve any decisions. Then, instead of naming just one person to hold your power of attorney, you will name two. Both signatures will be required to exercise any of the listed powers. It is typical for spouses to name each other as the primary and sole holder of the power of attorney. But in case both spouses should become incapacitated, they name two or more of their children as substitute or successor holders of the power of attorney.

You could name three, four, five, or more persons to act. But there does come a point where if you name too many people, it is unrealistic to expect the multiple power holders to agree, not to mention the logistics of obtaining everyone's signature. Sometime parents name all of their children as substitute or successor holders of the power of attorney because they don't want to hurt one or more child's feelings because he or she is excluded from the decisional process.

FACT

Family dynamics are often a consideration in deciding whom you want to name as your power of attorney. For instance, if it is a second marriage for you, you might not want your spouse to have sole authority over your property if you become incapacitated.

Creating a Power of Attorney

You can typically buy a power of attorney form at an office supply store and fill in the blanks. There are also numerous inexpensive computer software programs that will generate a power of attorney document. These programs allow you to insert your name, the name of the person or persons who will serve as your primary holder of the power of attorney, and name of the person or persons who will hold the power of attorney if the first person is not available. Then the programs typically generate a list of powers you can give to the holder of your power of attorney. You should always sign your power of attorney in the presence of two witnesses and a notary. Even if your state law does not require witnesses or a notary, it is a good idea to sign the document with the formalities that would meet the laws of any state.

ALERT!

Be certain that the power of attorney you create meets the requirements under your state law and that you understand the powers you are giving to the holder of your power of attorney.

You can make an appointment with a lawyer to prepare your power of attorney. Interview attorneys and ask how much it will cost to have the document prepared. Make sure to tell the lawyers that you are prepared with the names, addresses, and telephone numbers of the person or persons who will hold your power of attorney. Sometimes the lawyer will want everyone's social security number as well. You should also tell the lawyer that you have reviewed the powers, and you are prepared to let him or her know which powers you want included.

Chapter 21

Funeral Arrangements and Other Considerations

The most important thing you can do for your family is be prepared. By planning ahead and making as many decisions as you can, you are able to ease the burden of your loved ones after you pass on. However, your plan can only be implemented if your family knows a plan exists and where to locate the paperwork to carry out your plan.

Instructions for Your Family

It is important that you leave instructions for your family so they know what needs to be done if something were to happen to you. It is equally important that these instructions are clear and easy to find. The first thing you need to do is to get organized.

Chapter 2 provided you with step-by-step instructions on what information you need to gather about each piece of property you own. Throughout the rest of the book, you have been making decisions regarding what type of plan to create and what information and instructions to include within the plan. Hopefully your studies resulted in the creation a plan, and you have drafted documents that meet your wants and the needs of your loved ones.

It's not enough to just have a plan; you need to make sure that your family *knows* you have a plan. You don't have to tell your family exactly what your plan is, but they need to know that it exists. And, of course, your family needs to know where to find your documents and paperwork.

Where to Keep Your Documents

If your family can't find your will, trust, or your important paperwork, your property may not be distributed in the way you planned. Your family's first job after you are gone is to find your paperwork. This may not be as easy as it sounds. There are numerous places where you might keep your paperwork:

- In your house
- With your lawyer
- Filed with your local probate court
- In your safe-deposit box

There is no one right answer as to where you should keep your original documents and your important papers. After you have weighed the advantages and disadvantages of each option, make a decision and be sure to inform your family.

At Home

If you keep your original documents in your house, you need to make sure that your family knows where to find them. You may think your desk or home office is very organized, but everybody has a different filing system. What makes sense to you may not be what your family expected.

If you keep your original documents at home, you run the risk that if something happens to your house, your documents will be destroyed. This isn't very likely, but it could happen. Or perhaps you think that because your spouse knows how to find your documents, you are prepared. If something happens to both you and your spouse, the rest of the family might not know where to look.

The notebook is a highly recommended method of staying organized. Your original documents can be neatly placed in your notebook, along with your other important papers. If something happens, your family will know exactly where to look.

If you have been keeping your documents in a safe-deposit box, you need to read the section later in this chapter about safe-deposit boxes. You may change your mind about keeping your important documents there.

With the Lawyer

You could leave your original documents with your lawyer. Your lawyer will be happy to keep your original will or trust, but he or she is unlikely to want to become the custodian of your other important documents, such as your life insurance policies, annuities, information about your financial accounts, or investments. Also, when you leave your original documents with your lawyer, your family typically feels obliged to hire that lawyer to handle your affairs after you are gone.

Filed with the Probate Court

If you have a will, you can place the original on deposit with your local probate court. This prevents anyone from tampering with your will, and your family will have easy access to the document after you are gone. However, your local probate court will not become the custodian of your other important papers.

Safe-Deposit Boxes

There are many practical issues regarding a safe-deposit box that you might not have considered. Although the purpose of a safe-deposit box is to have a place that is secure to keep important papers or valuable items, a safe-deposit box can be difficult to access if you are incapacitated or gone.

Giving Out Keys

The first issue involves who has keys to your safe-deposit box. Even if you have filled out the proper forms at your bank or the location of your safe-deposit box to give someone else access to your box, the person you authorize can't get into the safe-deposit box without being charged, unless they have a key or know where to locate your key.

Obviously, you need to let your family know where you keep the keys. If your family can't find your keys, the person authorized to enter your safe-deposit box can access the box, but the cost of opening a safe-deposit box without a key is $100 to $150. You can save your family this frustration and expense by being prepared.

Authorizing Access

As stated before, you can authorize someone to have access to your safe-deposit box. However, you should carefully consider this decision. If you and your spouse are the only ones authorized to open the box and you are both gone, it will be very difficult for your family to gain access to your important documents. It is a good idea to list another person besides your spouse to have access to your box. If you are worried and don't want anyone besides your spouse to have access, you will just have to run the risk that it will be more difficult if something happens to the both of you.

If there is no one living to open your safe-deposit box, your family is going to have to get a court order to gain access. Your local probate court judge typically enters the order. The person who needs to obtain the court order is the executor you named in your will. However, before your executor can get a court order to open your safe-deposit box, he has to have your original will. He will then need to open your estate, have himself appointed as executor, and seek a probate court order directing the bank to allow him access to your safe-deposit box. This process can take a while.

If your executor cannot locate your will, but believes that you have a will in your safe-deposit box and that he is appointed as executor, then he will need to file a request with your local probate court to obtain an order for the limited purpose of opening your safe-deposit box to look for your will. If the will is not found, then he will need to petition to open a probate proceeding following the procedures for a person who died without a will. Then, after this person is appointed as your executor, he will file a petition to have full access to your safe-deposit box.

As you can see, if you have not provided the bank or credit union with the proper authorization to give someone access, it is very difficult, time-consuming, and expensive to gain access to your safe-deposit box!

You might consider putting your will in your safe-deposit box and limiting the number of persons who have access to it. After you are gone, the person you give access to your safe-deposit box will have plenty of time to open the box, find your will, and initiate the process to probate your estate.

Documents to Keep in a Safe-Deposit Box

It is highly recommended you keep a notebook as described in Chapter 2. If you organize all of your important information in one three-ring binder or notebook, you can put it into your safe-deposit box. Your notebook will contain:

- The original deed to your real estate
- Title to your vehicles or boats
- Original stock certificates
- Bonds
- Certificate of deposit
- Life insurance policies
- Annuity contracts

If you don't like the concept of using a notebook, you could put each of these documents in one or more envelopes and put the envelopes in your safe-deposit box. When you keep original documents in your safe-deposit box, you don't have to worry about the documents being lost or destroyed. You just need to make sure someone has access to the box after you are gone.

You should never keep your original medical designate or living will in your safe-deposit box. These are documents that need to be available in the event of a medical emergency. Your medical designate is the document that authorized someone to make medical decisions on your behalf, and your living will provides the instructions about whether or not you want your life artificially prolonged. If these documents are not available because either the bank or credit union is not open or your family is having difficulty gaining access to your safe-deposit box, the wrong decisions might be made about your medical care. An original medical designate and living will should be immediately available to the person you have named to make those choices on your behalf.

Prepayment Plans

You can make all of the selections about your final arrangements and prepay for the funeral and burial or cremation. What most people don't realize is that making these arrangements on a prepayment plan, is much cheaper.

By creating a prepayment plan, you will be able to make all of the decisions and not leave your family guessing or wondering about what you wanted. You would be surprised how many choices there are about funeral arrangements. Your family won't know if you wanted a $2,000 funeral or a $20,000 funeral unless you tell them.

If you pay for your arrangements in advance, you need to put the paperwork confirming the payment where your family can find the information. If you don't want to pay for your funeral arrangements before you are gone, you should at least make sure that you have left clear instructions about what you want. Again, the more specific you can be, the easier it will be for your family.

Your instructions are not typically included in your will or trust. Therefore, your instructions should be handwritten or typed and left with your other important documents. If you are keeping a notebook as an organizational system, this would be the perfect place to store your instructions.

FACT

The average funeral can range in cost from $3,000 to $12,000. Families often feel guilty wondering how much you wanted them to spend. Help out. Give your family some direction.

Funeral or Cremation Instructions

If you don't want to create a prepayment plan, you can still ease the emotional burden on your loved ones by making decisions and leaving instructions regarding your wishes for funeral or cremation arrangements. While this is probably the last thing you want to think about, your family will never know what you truly wanted if you don't tell them. At the very least, you should let them know whether you would prefer a funeral and burial or cremation. If you want to be more specific than that, there are plenty of other decisions to be made.

Funeral and Burial

If you want a funeral and burial when you die, the major decisions should be made first. For instance, you might first decide if the burial will be in-ground or aboveground entombment. Next is where the burial will take place. It's likely that you will know of a cemetery in which you would like a plot. Perhaps you have family and friends who have already passed away and want to have the same final resting place. Then you will probably want to decide on a funeral home. You could even shop around to find which funeral home would provide the best services for the best price.

Other decisions you may want to make include:

- Who you wish to be pallbearers
- What type of casket you prefer
- Whether you want an open or closed casket
- If you would prefer to have the funeral service in a location other than the funeral home
- Name of the clergy you want to preside over the service
- What you want to be buried in (clothing, jewelry, etc.)
- What music you want to be played at the service
- Specific biblical passages or literature you want read
- Who you want to do the readings
- Instructions regarding flower arrangements

Of course, there are other instructions that can be left for your loved ones. How detailed you want to be is entirely up to you, but remember that the more decisions you make for your family, the easier it will be on all involved.

Cremation

Though cremation is becoming more common, many families still do not accept it as a proper process. If you want to be cremated, it's best to discuss it with your family in addition to leaving instructions. If you do not discuss it and make your reasons known, some family members may fight against it when you die.

The decisions you make regarding cremation are very similar to those made for a funeral and burial. However, one major decision that may be considered is what you want done with your remains. You can have them all placed into one urn, you can request that they be scattered in a specific location, or you can even have them divided up among certain people. Keep in mind, however, that your family members may have difficulty scattering your remains. You will likely want to include this topic in your discussion with the family.

Most cremations include a memorial service of some type. You can be as specific as you want regarding the service, if you want one. Some services allow the family members to view the body before it is cremated; others simply have pictures and belongings on display. Take a look at the list of considerations regarding the funeral service and see if any apply to the service you have in mind for cremation.

Organ Donations

If you would like to donate any of your organs, you should leave your family instructions regarding your intentions. There is a uniform donor card you can complete at ✐ *www.shareyourlife.org/become_donor_card.pdf.* There is also a uniform notification to your family that lets them know your wishes about donating your organs. You will find that form by visiting ✐ *www.shareyourlife.org/become_notifi_form.pdf.* Of course, you don't have to use these forms.

FACT

Many states include your intentions about organ donations on your driver's license. It is very likely that you would have your driver's license with you if it were necessary to make a decision about an organ transplant.

You can prepare a paper that states your name and lists the organs you would like donated, and sign the paper in the presence of two witnesses. Although many states do not require a notary, it's a good idea to sign in the presence of two witnesses and a notary. Then, make sure you have informed your family about what you want done. So many times if the desired organ is not preserved shortly after your death, your intentions will not be met because it will not be medically possible to preserve the organ while your family finds your organ transplant instructions. Ⓔ

Appendices

Glossary

annuitant

The person, usually the owner of the annuity, who receives the annuity payouts.

annuity

A contract or agreement between you and the issuing company. You give the issuing company a certain amount of money, and in turn it promises to invest your money and repay you according to the option or payment method that you choose.

articles

The parts of a will. Each article is designed to accomplish a purpose.

beneficiary

The person for whose benefit a trust is created. The person named to receive your life insurance, annuity, or retirement plan.

codicil

An amendment to a will.

cost basis

The amount you subtract from the sale price of a property to compute your gain or loss when you sell a piece of property.

creditor

Any person or entity to whom you owe money.

credit shelter trust

A trust; usually created within a revocable trust that typically places the estate tax exemption amount into a trust for the benefit of the surviving spouse.

death tax

The tax your estate might owe when you die.

devise

A transfer of property after your death by your will.

devisee

The person or organization to whom you transfer property in your will.

executor

The person you name to carry out the instructions in your will. In some states the executor is called a personal representative.

exemption equivalent

The government grants a tax credit equal to a specified amount, the exemption equivalent. The exemption equivalent is currently

$1,000,000. This is often referred to as a "piggy bank" throughout the book.

gift
A voluntary transfer of property without receiving payment.

gift tax exclusion
The amount of money or property you can give each year.

grantor
The person who creates a trust; also known as settlor or creator.

grantor retained annuity trust
A sophisticated tax-planning device that allows you to make a gift at a discounted value; often referred to as GRAT.

group life insurance
Typically term insurance offered through your place of employment. As a member of the employer's group, you are entitled to a stated amount of insurance benefits paid to the beneficiary or beneficiaries you name.

guardian
The person you name in your will who has the power and duty to care for your minor child or children after you die.

heir
Any person who would receive your property if you died without a will.

intangible property
Property you cannot feel and touch. Intangible property represents evidence of ownership such as bank accounts, stocks, bonds, promissory notes, or property of a similar nature.

intestate
When a person dies without making a will or without leaving what her or his wishes were with respect to the disposal of property after her or his death.

intestate laws
Law each state has on how property will be distributed when someone dies without a will.

IRA
Individual Retirement Account; a retirement account that allows you to take advantage of tax-deferred contributions and/or growth or tax-free growth.

irrevocable trust
A trust that cannot be revoked or made void, canceled, rescinded, or reversed by anyone.

marital deduction
The right to subtract the value of property transferred to your surviving spouse, as long as you are leaving your spouse a qualified interest.

marital taxable base
The sum of the husband's taxable base and the wife's taxable base.

per capita

A method of dividing property in equal shares among a number of persons. If a named person is not alive, his or her share is divided equally among the other named persons who are living.

per stirpes

A method of dividing property whereby if the person to whom you have left property is not living, that person's share is divided in equal shares among his or her descendants.

personal property

All property other than real estate.

power of appointment

A person named in your trust document or will who has the power, upon your death, to alter the distribution of shares to the beneficiaries and/or to change the beneficiaries named in the document. There are two types of power of appointment: limited and general.

power of attorney

A legal document that gives the holder of the power of attorney the right to do something for you.

probate

The legal process to prove the validity of your will. Probate has become the word used to describe the entire legal process that occurs when a person dies with or without a will.

qualified personal residence trust

A sophisticated tax-reduction technique that allows you to transfer your personal residence to the next generation at a fraction of the transfer tax cost; often referred to as QPRT.

real property

Real estate including buildings, lots, and vacant land.

residual devise

When you leave the rest and remainder of your property, this is a residual devise. A residual devise is made in the residual clause of your will.

retainer

An amount of money the lawyer requires be placed on deposit before he or she starts a job.

revocable trust

A trust where you or someone you name is given the power to change or revoke the document.

settlor

The person who creates a trust. The settlor is often referred to as a grantor.

specific devise

When you leave specifically described property to a person or organization, you have made a specific devise.

successor beneficiaries
In a trust document, the persons you name who will enjoy the benefits of the property when you are gone.

successor trustee
A person or an entity you name to serve as trustee when you are gone.

tangible property
Property you can feel and touch.

taxable base
The property that is taxed when you die, along with the taxable gifts you made while living.

taxable gift
A gift made to any person above a certain amount per year.

testamentary trust
A trust that is contained inside of a will.

testate
When a person dies with a will.

trust
A legal document that transfers title of a property to an individual or entity for the benefit of another person or entity.

trust corpus
The property that you transfer into the name of a trust. Trust corpus is often called the trust principal.

trustee
The person or entity named to carry out the instructions contained in the trust document. The trustee also holds legal title to the trust property.

unlimited marital deduction
The right to give your spouse an unlimited amount of property without gift taxes.

will
The document that directs and instructs your executor or personal representative to distribute your property after you are gone.

Appendix B

Resources

Online Resources

✒ *www.legacywriter.com*
This is an Internet site that allows you to complete an easy-to-understand questionnaire that generates a will according to your answers.

✒ *www.videolaw.com*
This site is owned by the author, Kimberly A. Colgate. It provides a free library that guides you to relevant tax topics, IRS forms, and the law in all fifty states and markets videos on important tax and estate-planning issues.

✒ *www.nvo.com/finalplans*
This site has been online since 1998, but the company has been in business for twenty-five years. Finalplans.com provides invaluable information about how to make your final plans at an affordable price.

✒ *www.bestcase.com/statebar.htm*
This site will guide you to the state bar association in your state, which regulates lawyers. Each bar association site has different features, though most will guide you to a lawyer referral service regulated by the bar association.

Publications

Kiplinger's Personal Finance magazine is rich with articles on every conceivable estate-planning topic. The best way to access the archive of their publications is via their Web site at ✒ *www.kiplinger.com/magazine.*

"Estate Tax or No, You Still Need a Plan," by Ronaleen R. Roha (May 2001, *Kiplinger's Personal Finance*).

"Estate Planning Basics," by the National Association of Financial and Estate Planning. The article can be found online at ✒ *www.nafep.com/estate_planning/default.asp* or by contacting the National Association of Financial and Estate Planning at 525 E. 4500 South, #F-100, Salt Lake City, UT 84107; phone: (801) 266-9900; fax: (801) 266-1019; e-mail: *nafep@nafep.com.*

An outstanding resource of hundreds of estate-planning articles can be found online at: ✒ *http://moneycentral.msn.com/retire/articles/homedept.asp.* Categories include: Create Your Plan, Invest for Retirement, Plan Your Estate, Minimize Estate Taxes, and more.

Living & Dying with Your IRA and Other Retirement Plans, by Bill Wolfkiel, is specifically written for IRA participants with account balances of over $750,000 and large estate holders with additional assets. It is an easy-to-use, in-depth manual with many actual supported cases and applicable IRS regulations included as endnotes.

Asset Inventory Worksheet

FAMILY INFORMATION

Your legal name: _____

Social Security number: _____ Date of birth: _____

Your spouse's name:_____

Social Security number: _____ Date of birth: _____

Date of marriage: _____

State of residency: _____ U.S. citizen? Yes _____ No _____

Former spouse(s): _____

Date of divorce(s): _____

Terms of divorce or separation (if any of the terms of the divorce or separation are applicable to your current estate): _____

Parents (if living): _____

Information about your children and grandchildren

Child 1:_____ Social Security #:_____

Dependent? _____ Birth date: _____ Married: _____

Address: _____

Does your child have any children?

Names of grandchildren:_____

Child 2:_____ Social security #: _____

Dependent? _____ Birth date: _____ Married: _____

Address: _____

Does your child have any children?

Names of grandchildren:_____

Insert a page including the information about additional children.

ADVISORS

List the name, address, and telephone number for each.

Attorney: _____

Accountant: _____

Banker: _____

Insurance agent: _____

Investment advisor: _____

Stockbroker: _____

Trust officer: _____

Others: _____

ASSET INFORMATION
REAL ESTATE
Property I

Please place a copy of all deeds in your estate-planning organizer.

Address: _____

Personal residence? (Primary or secondary, and period of occupancy and ownership):

_____

Owned in name of: _____

Form of ownership: _____

Date of purchase: _____

How acquired (gift, purchase, etc.): _____

Cost: _____

Current market value: _____

Debt on property: _____

Name of debt holder: _____

Amount of remaining debt: _____

Monthly payments (principal and interest): _____

Annual taxes: _____

Insert an additional page for each piece of real estate.

CASH

	Bank Name	Husband's	Wife's	Joint
Checking account	_____	_____	_____	_____
Balance	_____	_____	_____	_____
Savings account	_____	_____	_____	_____
Balance	_____	_____	_____	_____
Certificates of deposit	_____	_____	_____	_____
Balance	_____	_____	_____	_____
TOTAL	_____	_____	_____	_____

STOCKS

Description	Ownership	# of Shares	Cost Basis	Acquisition Date	December 31, 20__ Value	Current Value	Annual Dividend
_____	_____	_____	_____	_____	_____	_____	_____
_____	_____	_____	_____	_____	_____	_____	_____
_____	_____	_____	_____	_____	_____	_____	_____
_____	_____	_____	_____	_____	_____	_____	_____
_____	_____	_____	_____	_____	_____	_____	_____
_____	_____	_____	_____	_____	_____	_____	_____
_____	_____	_____	_____	_____	_____	_____	_____
_____	_____	_____	_____	_____	_____	_____	_____
				Totals	$ _____	$ _____	

Insert additional pages as needed.

BONDS

Description	Ownership	# of Shares	Cost Basis	Acquisition Date	December 31, 20__ Value	Current Value	Annual Dividend
_____	_____	_____	_____	_____	_____	_____	_____
_____	_____	_____	_____	_____	_____	_____	_____
_____	_____	_____	_____	_____	_____	_____	_____
_____	_____	_____	_____	_____	_____	_____	_____
_____	_____	_____	_____	_____	_____	_____	_____
_____	_____	_____	_____	_____	_____	_____	_____
_____	_____	_____	_____	_____	_____	_____	_____
_____	_____	_____	_____	_____	_____	_____	_____
_____	_____	_____	_____	_____	_____	_____	_____

Totals $ _____ $ _____

Insert additional pages as needed.

MUTUAL FUNDS

Name of fund: _____

Value of fund: _____

Cost basis of fund: _____

Name of fund: _____

Value of fund: _____

Cost basis of fund: _____

Insert an additional page for each fund owned.

LIFE INSURANCE

Company: _____ Policy number: _____

Address: _____

Type of policy: _____ Face amount: _____

Ownership rights: _____

Beneficiary designation: _____

Cash value: _____ Cash value at retirement: _____

Annual premiums: _____ Paid by: _____

Settlement options: _____

Where is your original policy located? _____

Insert an additional page for each life insurance policy owned.

EMPLOYEE BENEFITS

Employer: _____

Address: _____

Type of plan: _____

Value of current plan: _____

Retirement benefits: _____

Death benefits: _____

How to contact the plan administrator: _____ Telephone number: _____

Where is the information about your plan located? _____

INDIVIDUAL RETIREMENT ACCOUNTS

Your IRA

Location of benefits (bank or custodial name): _____

Value of current plan: _____

Retirement benefits: _____

Death benefits: _____

Where is the information about your IRA located? _____

Your Spouse's IRA

Location of benefits (bank or custodial name): _____

Value of current plan: _____

Retirement benefits: _____

Death benefits: _____

Where is the information about this IRA located? _____

If you and your spouse have multiple IRAs, provide the requested information about each IRA.

SOCIAL SECURITY

Estimated basic Social Security benefit for:

Husband: _____

Wife: _____

Do you receive any other retirement or death benefits?

Private: _____

Employer: _____

Banks or credit card death benefits: _____

<u>MISCELLANEOUS ASSETS</u>

Please enter a dollar amount in the following table for each item that applies to your family.

Item	*Husband*	*Wife*	*Joint*
Furniture	$ _____	$ _____	$ _____
Automobiles	_____	_____	_____
Jewelry	_____	_____	_____
Artwork	_____	_____	_____
Boats	_____	_____	_____
Other: _____	_____	_____	_____
Other: _____	_____	_____	_____
Other: _____	_____	_____	_____

<u>LIABILITIES</u>
<u>OTHER THAN LIABILITIES ON REAL ESTATE</u>

Name of creditor: _____ Due date: _____ Balance owing: _____
Address: _____
Account number:_____

Name of creditor: _____ Due date: _____ Balance owing: _____
Address: _____
Account number:_____

Name of creditor: _____ Due date: _____ Balance owing: _____
Address: _____
Account number:_____

Name of creditor: _____ Due date: _____ Balance owing: _____
Address: _____
Account number:_____

SUMMARY OF ASSETS AND LIABILITIES

ASSETS

Enter a dollar amount for each asset in the following table.

Asset	Husband	Wife	Joint
Cash	$ _____	$ _____	$ _____
Stocks	_____	_____	_____
Bonds	_____	_____	_____
Mutual funds	_____	_____	_____
Real estate	_____	_____	_____
Personal residence	_____	_____	_____
Life insurance	_____	_____	_____
Employee benefits	_____	_____	_____
Miscellaneous assets	_____	_____	_____

LIABILITIES

Enter a dollar amount for each liability in the following table.

Liability	Husband	Wife	Joint
Real estate	$ _____	$ _____	$ _____
Other bank debt	_____	_____	_____
Credit cards	_____	_____	_____
Taxes	_____	_____	_____
Other debt	_____	_____	_____

Appendix D

Sample Trust

Articles I–VI are reproduced and described in Chapter 14. The remaining portion of the trust document contains provisions that are standard to most trust documents.

ARTICLE VII
POWERS OF TRUSTEE AND OTHER PROVISIONS

7.1 <u>Powers of Trustee.</u> In the administration of this Trust, the Trustee shall have the following powers, in addition to and not in limitation of the Trustee's common law powers and statutory powers, provided (1) that such common law and statutory powers shall only be exercised to the extent they are not in conflict with the provisions of this Article and (2) that such common law and statutory powers shall be exercised in a fiduciary capacity in accordance with the general standards of trust administration imposed upon trustees.

(a) To receive and retain the initial Trust corpus and all other property which I may transfer to the Trustee either during my lifetime, by Will or other testamentary disposition, or which any other person may hereafter transfer to the Trustee. The Trustee shall receive all such property as part of the Trust even though it may not be a legal investment for the Trustee and even though such property by reason of its character may not be an appropriate trust investment apart from this provision. The Trustee is authorized to retain its own stock or other securities or stock or securities of any affiliate or holding company that owns the Trustee.

(b) To sell, exchange, give options upon, partition, or otherwise dispose of any property that the Trustee may hold from time to time, at public or private sale, or otherwise, for cash or other consideration or on credit, and upon such terms and for such consideration as the Trustee deems advisable; and to transfer and convey such property free of all trust.

(c) To invest and reinvest in any property, real or personal, including (without limiting the generality of the foregoing language) securities of domestic and foreign corporations and investment trusts, bonds, preferred stocks, common stocks, option contracts, "short sales," mortgages and mortgage participations, even though such investment by reason of its character, amount, proportion to the total trust estate, or otherwise would not be considered appropriate for a fiduciary apart from this provision, and even though such investment causes a greater proportion of the total trust to be invested in investments of one type or of one company than would be considered appropriate for a fiduciary apart from this provision. Such investment may be on a cash or margin basis, and the Trustee, for such purpose, may maintain and operate cash or margin accounts with brokers, and may deliver and pledge securities held or purchased by the Trustee with such brokers both as security for loans and advances made to the Trustee and to ensure the ability of the Trustee to deliver stock against short options. In addition, the Trustee may purchase life insurance even though it is non-income-producing. The Trustee is authorized to invest in any common fund, legal or discretionary, which may be operated by and/or under the control of a corporate Trustee.

(d) To make loans, secured or unsecured, in such amounts, upon such terms, at such rates of interest, and to such persons, trusts, corporations, or other parties as the Trustee deems advisable.

(e) To improve real estate, including the power to demolish buildings in whole or in part and to erect new buildings; to lease (including leasing for oil, gas, and minerals) real estate on such terms as the Trustee deems advisable, including the power to give leases for periods that extend beyond the duration of any trust; to foreclose, extend, assign, partially release, and discharge mortgages.

(f) To collect, pay, contest, compromise, or abandon, upon such terms and evidence as the Trustee deems advisable, any claims, including taxes, either in favor of or against trust property or the Trustee; to abandon or surrender any property.

(g) To employ brokers, banks, custodians, investment counsel, attorneys, accountants, and other agents, and to delegate to them such duties, rights, and powers of the Trustee (including the right to vote shares of stock held by the Trustee) for such periods as the Trustee deems advisable.

(h) To hold and register securities in the name of a nominee with or without the addition of words indicating such securities are held in a fiduciary capacity; to hold and register securities in a securities depository or in any other form convenient for the Trustee.

(i) To participate in any voting trust, merger, reorganization, consolidation, or liquidation affecting trust property and, in connection therewith, to deposit any trust property with or under the direction of any protective committee and to exchange any trust property for other property.

(j) To exercise any stock or other kind of option.

(k) To keep trust property in **Florida** or elsewhere, or with a depository or custodian.

(l) To determine (reasonably and in accordance with sound trust accounting principles) as to all sums of money or other things of value received by the Trustee, whether and to what extent the same shall be deemed to be principal or to be income, and as to all charges or expenses paid by the Trustee, whether and to what extent the same shall be charged against principal or against income, including the power to apportion any receipt or expense between principal and income and to determine what part, if any, of the actual income received upon any wasting investment or upon any security purchased or acquired at a premium shall be retained and added to principal to prevent a diminution of principal upon exhaustion or maturity thereof. The Trustee may also establish reserves for depreciation and anticipated expenses and fund such reserves for depreciation and anticipated expenses with appropriate charges against income. All determinations made pursuant to this subparagraph by the Trustee shall be made fairly to balance the interest of the income beneficiary and the remaindermen. The Trustee shall resolve all doubtful questions in favor of the income beneficiary. If an income beneficiary also serves as one of the Trustees of the Trust, then the income beneficiary–Trustee shall not exercise any of the powers granted by this subparagraph and all such powers shall be exercised by the other Trustee(s) only.

(m) To distribute the trust estate in cash or in kind, or partly in cash and partly in kind, as the Trustee deems advisable, and for purposes of distribution, to value the assets reasonably and in good faith as of the date of distribution. Such valuation shall be conclusive on all beneficiaries. The Trustee shall not be required to distribute a proportionate amount of each asset to each beneficiary but may instead make non-pro-rata distributions. In making distribution, the Trustee may, but shall not be required to, take account of the income tax basis in relation to market value of assets distributed. Distribution may be made directly to the beneficiary, to a legally appointed Guardian or Conservator or, where permitted by law, to a custodian under any Uniform Gifts to Minors Act, including a custodian selected by the Trustee.

(n) To deposit monies to be paid to a beneficiary who is a minor in any demand, savings bank, or savings and loan account maintained in the sole name of the minor and to accept the deposit receipt as a full acquittance.

(o) To accept the receipt of a minor as a full acquittance.

(p) To borrow from anyone (including the Trustee or any affiliate) in the name of the Trust, to execute promissory notes therefore and to secure obligations by mortgage or pledge of trust property, provided the Trustee shall not be personally liable and that any such loan shall be payable out of trust assets only.

(q) To hold, manage, invest, and account for any separate trust in one or more consolidated funds, in whole or in part, as the Trustee deems advisable. As to each consolidated fund, the division into the various shares comprising such a fund needs to be made only on the Trustee's books of account, in which each separate trust shall be allocated its proportionate share of principal and income of the fund and charged with its proportionate share of the expenses. No such holding shall defer any distribution.

(r) To carry, at the expense of the Trust, insurance of such kinds and in such amounts as the Trustee deems advisable to protect the trust estate and the Trustee personally against any hazard or liability.

(s) To exercise all of these powers without application to any court.

7.2 Diversification. The Trustee shall not be required to diversify assets and is authorized to receive and retain in the Trust any one or more securities or other property, whether or not such security or other property shall constitute a larger share of the Trust than would be appropriate for a fiduciary to receive and retain apart from this provision.

7.3 <u>Receipt.</u> No purchaser or other person dealing with the Trustee shall be responsible for the application of any money or other thing of value paid or delivered to the Trustee, and no purchaser or other person dealing with the Trustee and no issuer, transfer agent, or other agent dealing with the Trustee shall be under any obligation to ascertain or inquire into the power of the Trustee to purchase, sell, exchange, transfer, mortgage, pledge, distribute, or otherwise in any manner dispose of or deal with any property held by the Trustee. The Certificate of the Trustee that the Trustee is acting in conformance with the terms of this Agreement shall protect all persons dealing with the Trustee.

7.4 <u>Creditors Clause and Spendthrift Provision.</u> With respect to all payments and distributions to be made pursuant to the trusts established hereunder, no beneficiary shall have any right to or interest in the income or principal therefrom until the same has been paid to him or her. Both principal and income of such trusts shall be free from the interference and control of the creditors of any beneficiary and neither the principal nor income of such trusts shall be subject to assignment or other anticipation by any beneficiary unless the Trustee determines that such assignment or anticipation is clearly and unequivocally in the best interest of such beneficiary. Both principal and income of such trusts shall be free from seizure under any legal, equitable, or other process whatsoever. If the Trustee believes the foregoing may be violated or if the Trustee believes the protection of any beneficiary requires it, the Trustee may withhold any part or all of the income and principal payments to which a beneficiary may be entitled and use and pay directly such portion thereof as the Trustee deems advisable.

7.5 <u>Corporate Merger.</u> If the Trustee merges or consolidates, the corporation formed by such merger or consolidation shall act as Trustee and shall possess and exercise all powers and authority herein provided.

7.6 <u>Exculpatory.</u> No successor Trustee shall be liable for any act or failure to act of any predecessor Trustee. With the approval of the person making the appointment of the Trustee, the successor Trustee shall not be required to review the accounts, acts, or omissions of predecessor Trustees or to take action against predecessor Trustees for breaches of trust and may accept whatever assets are turned over without further inquiry.

7.7 <u>Construction.</u> This Agreement, all trusts established hereunder, all powers of appointment, and all other matters shall be constructed under and regulated by **Florida** law. The validity of this Agreement and all trusts established hereunder shall be determined by **Florida** law.

7.8 <u>Notices.</u> All notices required or permitted hereunder shall be in writing and sent by ordinary mail to the recipient at such address as may be specified from time to time. If any person receiving notice shall be a minor or under other legal disability, a living parent, guardian, or other person having physical custody of such person may act for such person in receiving notice. Nothing contained in this paragraph shall be deemed to give such person acting in conjunction with the Trustee the power or right to enlarge, shift, or restrict the beneficial interest of any beneficiary of any Trust.

7.9 <u>Reduction or Release of Powers.</u> I give to the Trustee the power to release or renounce any power, privilege, or right (including this power) or the power to reduce the scope and extent of any power, privilege, or right (including this power). If there is more than one Trustee of this Trust, this power may be exercised by any one Trustee individually or by all of the Trustees collectively.

7.10 <u>Tax Elections.</u> The Trustee shall have the power to select tax years and make, or refrain from making, all other decisions and elections permitted under any applicable income, estate, or inheritance tax law, including the imposition of a lien on Family Trust assets to secure tax payments, without regard to the effect thereof, if any, on any beneficiary of this Trust and, if any such decision or election shall be made, to apportion or refrain from apportioning the consequences thereof among the respective interests of the beneficiaries of this Trust, all in such manner as the Trustee shall deem appropriate. If the Trustee is responsible for preparing and filing a federal estate tax return in my estate, and determines there is uncertainty as to the inclusion of a particular item of property in my gross estate for federal estate tax purposes, then such property may, in the discretion of the Trustee, be excluded from my gross estate in my federal estate tax return. Similarly, if the Trustee is responsible for preparing and filing a federal estate tax return in my estate, then the decision of the Trustee as to the valuation date for federal estate tax purposes shall be conclusive on all concerned.

7.11 <u>Termination of Trusts.</u> Notwithstanding any other provision of this Agreement, no trust or interest in a trust created pursuant to this Agreement or any trust or interest established by the exercise of a power of appointment shall (1) continue to remain contingent beyond twenty-one (21) years after the death of the last to die of any beneficiary who is living on the date on which this Trust becomes irrevocable, or (2) continue beyond the time at which their continued existence would violate the Rule Against Perpetuities. Upon the expiration of either of these periods, any trust or interest in a trust or any trust or interest established by the exercise of power of appointment shall terminate and the assets thereof shall be distributed outright in equal shares to the income beneficiaries thereof, or if any income beneficiary shall be deceased, that beneficiary's shares to his or her descendants per stirpes.

7.12 <u>Loans and Purchases.</u> The Trustee may utilize funds contained in the Family Trust, at the Trustee's discretion, to purchase assets from my estate and/or my wife's estate and/or to lend sums of money to the Personal Representative of either of same estates in order that cash may be made available to said estates. It is my intent by this provision to specifically authorize such purchases or loans even though the Personal Representative of said estates and the Trustee may be the same person(s) or corporation(s).

7.13 <u>Captions</u>. The captions in this Agreement are for convenience only and shall not be considered as part of this Agreement or in any way limiting or amplifying the terms and provisions hereof.

7.14 <u>Severability</u>. If any provision of this Agreement shall be invalid or unenforceable, the remaining provisions shall have full force and effect.

7.15 <u>Exercise of Rights</u>. All rights (such as release, disclaimer, and renunciation) exercisable by any beneficiary shall be exercised by delivery to the Trustee of a writing, signed and acknowledged by the person exercising such right. All notices, certificates, and other communications permitted or required hereunder shall be in writing.

ARTICLE VIII
ACCOUNTING

Except to the extent otherwise excused by governing law, the Trustee shall keep the presently vested beneficiaries of the Trust reasonably informed of the Trust and its administration. Within thirty (30) days after my death, the Trustee shall inform in writing the presently vested beneficiaries of its name and address and of their right to request and receive a copy of the terms of the Trust that describe or affect their interest, and relevant information about the assets and administration of the Trust. The Trustee shall render annually, or as soon thereafter as reasonably practicable, and send to me or my guardian during my lifetime and after my death to each presently vested beneficiary, an annual accounting statement showing all receipts, disbursements, and distributions for the preceding year, together with a statement of all of the property then in the Trustee's possession belonging to the Trust. Such annual accounting statement shall be approved and be final and binding on me and on each presently vested beneficiary (1) when the same is approved in writing by such beneficiary or (2) unless a proceeding to raise an objection to the accounting statement is commenced within six (6) months after the date of sending by ordinary mail, or the delivery, of such annual accounting statement.

Upon termination of any Trust, the Trustee shall render and send to all beneficiaries a final accounting statement showing all receipts, disbursements, and distributions since my death, together with a statement of all the property then in the Trustee's possession and belonging to the Trust. Such final accounting statement shall be approved and be final and binding on each beneficiary (1) when the same is approved in writing by such beneficiary or (2) unless a proceeding to raise an objection to the accounting statement is commenced within six (6) months after the date of sending by ordinary mail, or the delivery of, such annual accounting statement. After approval of the final accounting statement and the payment of all the obligations of the Trust and distribution of the principal and accumulated net income of the Trust to the beneficiaries entitled to the same, the Trustee shall be released and discharged from all liability for the Trustee's acts and obligations under this Agreement. If an accounting statement is objected to as provided herein, the objection shall be heard and decided by the probate court in the county where the corporate Trustee is located.

If any beneficiary shall be a minor or under other legal disability, a living parent, guardian, or other person having physical custody of such beneficiary may act for such beneficiary in approving accounts with the same effect as if such beneficiary had been of full age or without legal disability, and had for himself approved such accounts. Nothing contained in this paragraph shall be deemed to give such person acting in conjunction with the Trustee the power or right to enlarge, shift, or restrict the beneficial interest of any beneficiary of any trust.

The books and records of the Trustee relating to duties as Trustee of this Trust shall be open during business hours for inspection by me or any beneficiary of this Trust or their duly-appointed attorney, accountant, agent, or other representative.

IN WITNESS WHEREOF, we have hereunto set our hands and seals as of this _____ day of _____, 200___. Signed in the presence of:

Witnesses:

_____

Witness #1

_____

Witness #2

_____
Insert your name
Settlor-Trustee

AFFIDAVIT OF EXECUTION

STATE OF _____)

) SS.

COUNTY OF _____)

On this _____ day of _____, 200__, before me personally appeared (insert your name), who being duly sworn, says that she has read the foregoing Trust by her signed as Settlor-Trustee and knows the contents thereof.

On this _____ day of _____, 200__, before me personally appeared the two witnesses (insert name of witness #1) and (insert name of witness #2) who, in the Settlor-Trustee's presence and the presence of each other, witnessed the Settlor-Trustee execute her Revocable Trust. They believe (insert your name) to be of sound mind.

                                         _____

                                         Notary Public

                                         Sarasota County, Florida

                                         My commission expires: _____

Index

A

Affidavit of Execution, 92
Annuitant, 172
Annuities, 171–80
  advantages, 179–80
  beneficiaries, 53
  cost basis of, 176–77
  death tax and, 177–78, 194–95
  defined, 172–73
  disadvantages, 179–80
  early withdrawal penalties,
    175–76
  evaluating, 178–80
  investment choices, 173
  overriding wills, 16, 33, 53
  probate and, 38, 46, 53,
    173–74
  tax implications, 174–76,
    177–78, 194–95
  trusts and, 123
  wills and, 16, 33, 53
Articles, 56
Asset distribution
  changing wills, 94–95
  combination instructions,
    76–77
  current distributions, 127
  dead beneficiaries and, 52, 63,
    64, 151, 152–55
  decisions, 18–19, 72, 74–77
  delayed distributions, 127–28
  disputes. *See* Distribution
    disagreements
  executor decisions, 72
  general instructions, 76, 132
  to minors. *See* Minors
  penalties, 129
  restrictions, 129–30
  specific instructions, 74–75,
    131–32

  specifying heirs. *See* Heirs
  timing, 127–29, 130–34, 153–56
  tools for, 30–32
  triggering events, 128–29
  trust example, 152–56
  "who" list, 17, 30–31, 73–74,
    94–95, 126
Assets
  cost basis of, 106–7, 108–11,
    188
  creditor protection, 7–8, 22
  notebook summarizing, 16–19,
    28–29, 43, 109, 122, 233–34
  planning inventory, 30, 245–52
  valuation, 17–18, 29, 106–7,
    108–9
  See also Joint property;
    Personal property; Property;
    Real estate

B

Bank accounts
  joint tenancy and, 105
  transferring, 122
  trusts and, 122
Beneficiaries
  annuity, 53
  confirming, 53
  dead, consequences of, 52,
    63, 64, 151, 152–55
  estates as, 51–52
  IRA, 16, 183–85
  life insurance, 16, 51–52,
    163–65
  successor beneficiaries, 50
  trust, 116–17, 152–56
  trustee duties to, 141, 159–60
Broad power of attorney, 216–17
Business contracts, 16

C

Charitable gifts, 199
Children
  defining, in wills, 58
  dividing property equally
    among, 30–31
  divorce of, 6, 73, 74, 126
  guardians for. *See* Guardians
  as IRA beneficiaries, 184–85
  maturity level considerations,
    6
  minors, 46, 78–80
  as multiple joint tenants, 48,
    111–12
  new babies, 2–3
  planning for, 6
  protecting inheritance of, 6,
    14, 26, 80
  remarriage issues, 5–6, 74,
    126, 183–84
  as successor co-trustees, 115
  trusts for, 14, 27, 80
  vying for executorship,
    39–40
Codicils, 98, 99, 102
College funding, 7, 26
Computer software, 84
Contesting wills. *See* Distribution
  disagreements
Continuing specific instructions,
  131–32
Contractual arrangements, 15–16,
  47
Cost basis
  annuities and, 176–77
  IRAs and, 188
  joint tenancy and, 106–7,
    108–11
  reduced, 108–9
  rules of, 106–7

THE EVERYTHING BUDGETING BOOK

By Tere Drenth

Filled with practical tips and advice you can use immediately, *The Everything® Budgeting Book* can be used time and time again as your life—and financial picture —changes. Whether you need to restructure debt, save for retirement, or are just looking for ways to trim costs on everyday expenses, this book will help you get in the black fast. Featuring seventy worksheets that you can copy and use over and over again, this user-friendly guide will help keep you financially healthy for years to come.

Trade paperback,
$14.95 ($22.95 CAN)
1-58062-786-2, 304 pages

OTHER *EVERYTHING*® BOOKS BY ADAMS MEDIA CORPORATION

BUSINESS

Everything® **Business Planning Book**
Everything® **Coaching & Mentoring Book**
Everything® **Home-Based Business Book**
Everything® **Leadership Book**
Everything® **Managing People Book**
Everything® **Network Marketing Book**
Everything® **Online Business Book**
Everything® **Project Management Book**
Everything® **Selling Book**
Everything® **Start Your Own Business Book**
Everything® **Time Management Book**

COMPUTERS

Everything® **Build Your Own Home Page Book**
Everything® **Computer Book**

Everything® **Internet Book**
Everything® **Microsoft® Word 2000 Book**

COOKING

Everything® **Barbecue Cookbook**
Everything® **Bartender's Book, $9.95**
Everything® **Chocolate Cookbook**
Everything® **Cookbook**
Everything® **Dessert Cookbook**
Everything® **Diabetes Cookbook**
Everything® **Low-Carb Cookbook**
Everything® **Low-Fat High-Flavor Cookbook**
Everything® **Mediterranean Cookbook**
Everything® **One-Pot Cookbook**
Everything® **Pasta Book**
Everything® **Quick Meals Cookbook**
Everything® **Slow Cooker Cookbook**

Everything® **Soup Cookbook**
Everything® **Thai Cookbook**
Everything® **Vegetarian Cookbook**
Everything® **Wine Book**

HEALTH

Everything® **Anti-Aging Book**
Everything® **Dieting Book**
Everything® **Herbal Remedies Book**
Everything® **Hypnosis Book**
Everything® **Menopause Book**
Everything® **Nutrition Book**
Everything® **Stress Management Book**
Everything®**Vitamins, Minerals, and Nutritional Supplements Book**

HISTORY

Everything® **American History Book**

Everything® **Civil War Book**
Everything® **World War II Book**

HOBBIES

Everything® **Bridge Book**
Everything® **Candlemaking Book**
Everything® **Casino Gambling Book**
Everything® **Chess Basics Book**
Everything® **Collectibles Book**
Everything® **Crossword and Puzzle Book**
Everything® **Digital Photography Book**
Everything® **Drums Book (with CD),**
    $19.95, ($31.95 CAN)
Everything® **Family Tree Book**
Everything® **Games Book**
Everything® **Guitar Book**
Everything® **Knitting Book**
Everything® **Magic Book**
Everything® **Motorcycle Book**
Everything® **Online Genealogy Book**
Everything® **Playing Piano and**
    Keyboards Book
Everything® **Rock & Blues Guitar**
    Book (with CD), $19.95,
    ($31.95 CAN)
Everything® **Scrapbooking Book**

HOME IMPROVEMENT

Everything® **Feng Shui Book**
Everything® **Gardening Book**
Everything® **Home Decorating Book**
Everything® **Landscaping Book**
Everything® **Lawn Care Book**
Everything® **Organize Your Home Book**

KIDS' STORY BOOKS

Everything® **Bedtime Story Book**
Everything® **Bible Stories Book**
Everything® **Fairy Tales Book**
Everything® **Mother Goose Book**

NEW AGE

Everything® **Astrology Book**

Everything® **Divining the Future Book**
Everything® **Dreams Book**
Everything® **Ghost Book**
Everything® **Meditation Book**
Everything® **Numerology Book**
Everything® **Palmistry Book**
Everything® **Spells and Charms Book**
Everything® **Tarot Book**
Everything® **Wicca and Witchcraft Book**

PARENTING

Everything® **Baby Names Book**
Everything® **Baby Shower Book**
Everything® **Baby's First Food Book**
Everything® **Baby's First Year Book**
Everything® **Breastfeeding Book**
Everything® **Get Ready for Baby Book**
Everything® **Homeschooling Book**
Everything® **Potty Training Book,**
    $9.95, ($15.95 CAN)
Everything® **Pregnancy Book**
Everything® **Pregnancy Organizer,**
    $15.00, ($22.95 CAN)
Everything® **Toddler Book**
Everything® **Tween Book**

PERSONAL FINANCE

Everything® **Budgeting Book**
Everything® **Get Out of Debt Book**
Everything® **Get Rich Book**
Everything® **Investing Book**
Everything® **Homebuying Book, 2nd Ed.**
Everything® **Homeselling Book**
Everything® **Money Book**
Everything® **Mutual Funds Book**
Everything® **Online Investing Book**
Everything® **Personal Finance Book**

PETS

Everything® **Cat Book**
Everything® **Dog Book**
Everything® **Dog Training and Tricks**
Everything® **Horse Book**
Everything® **Puppy Book**
Everything® **Tropical Fish Book**

REFERENCE

Everything® **Astronomy Book**
Everything® **Car Care Book**
Everything® **Christmas Book, $15.00,**
    ($21.95 CAN)
Everything® **Classical Mythology Book**
Everything® **Divorce Book**
Everything® **Etiquette Book**
Everything® **Great Thinkers Book**
Everything® **Learning French Book**
Everything® **Learning German Book**
Everything® **Learning Italian Book**
Everything® **Learning Latin Book**
Everything® **Learning Spanish Book**
Everything® **Mafia Book**
Everything® **Philosophy Book**
Everything® **Shakespeare Book**
Everything® **Tall Tales, Legends, &**
    Other Outrageous Lies Book
Everything® **Toasts Book**
Everything® **Trivia Book**
Everything® **Weather Book**
Everything® **Wills & Estate Planning**
    Book

RELIGION

Everything® **Angels Book**
Everything® **Buddhism Book**
Everything® **Catholicism Book**
Everything® **Judaism Book**
Everything® **Saints Book**
Everything® **World's Religions Book**
Everything® **Understanding Islam Book**

SCHOOL & CAREERS

Everything® **After College Book**
Everything® **College Survival Book**
Everything® **Cover Letter Book**
Everything® **Get-a-Job Book**
Everything® **Hot Careers Book**
Everything® **Job Interview Book**
Everything® **Online Job Search Book**
Everything® **Resume Book, 2nd Ed.**
Everything® **Study Book**

All Everything® books are priced at $12.95 or $14.95, unless otherwise stated. Prices subject to change without notice.
Canadian prices range from $11.95–$22.95 and are subject to change without notice.

WE HAVE EVERYTHING . . . .

SPORTS/FITNESS

Everything® **Bicycle Book**
Everything® **Fishing Book**
Everything® **Fly-Fishing Book**
Everything® **Golf Book**
Everything® **Golf Instruction Book**
Everything® **Pilates Book**
Everything® **Running Book**
Everything® **Sailing Book, 2nd Ed.**
Everything® **T'ai Chi and QiGong Book**
Everything® **Total Fitness Book**
Everything® **Weight Training Book**
Everything® **Yoga Book**

TRAVEL

Everything® **Guide to Las Vegas**
Everything® **Guide to New England**
Everything® **Guide to New York City**
Everything® **Guide to Washington D.C.**

Everything® **Travel Guide to The Disneyland Resort®, California Adventure®, Universal Studios®, and the Anaheim Area**
Everything® **Travel Guide to the Walt Disney World® Resort, Universal Studios®, and Greater Orlando, 3rd Ed.**

WEDDINGS & ROMANCE

Everything® **Creative Wedding Ideas Book**
Everything® **Dating Book**
Everything® **Jewish Wedding Book**
Everything® **Romance Book**
Everything® **Wedding Book, 2nd Ed.**
Everything® **Wedding Organizer, $15.00 ($22.95 CAN)**

Everything® **Wedding Checklist, $7.95 ($11.95 CAN)**
Everything® **Wedding Etiquette Book, $7.95 ($11.95 CAN)**
Everything® **Wedding Shower Book, $7.95 ($12.95 CAN)**
Everything® **Wedding Vows Book, $7.95 ($11.95 CAN)**
Everything® **Weddings on a Budget Book, $9.95 ($15.95 CAN)**

WRITING

Everything® **Creative Writing Book**
Everything® **Get Published Book**
Everything® **Grammar and Style Book**
Everything® **Grant Writing Book**
Everything® **Guide to Writing Children's Books**
Everything® **Writing Well Book**

ALSO AVAILABLE:
THE EVERYTHING® KIDS' SERIES!

Each book is 8" x 9¼", 144 pages, and two-color throughout.

Everything® **Kids' Baseball Book, 2nd Edition, $6.95** ($10.95 CAN)
Everything® **Kids' Bugs Book, $6.95** ($10.95 CAN)
Everything® **Kids' Cookbook, $6.95** ($10.95 CAN)
Everything® **Kids' Joke Book, $6.95** ($10.95 CAN)
Everything® **Kids' Math Puzzles Book, $6.95** ($10.95 CAN)
Everything® **Kids' Mazes Book, $6.95** ($10.95 CAN)
Everything® **Kids' Money Book, $6.95** ($11.95 CAN)

Everything® **Kids' Monsters Book, $6.95** ($10.95 CAN)
Everything® **Kids' Nature Book, $6.95** ($11.95 CAN)
Everything® **Kids' Puzzle Book $6.95,** ($10.95 CAN)
Everything® **Kids' Science Experiments Book, $6.95** ($10.95 CAN)
Everything® **Kids' Soccer Book, $6.95** ($10.95 CAN)
Everything® **Kids' Travel Activity Book, $6.95** ($10.95 CAN)

Available wherever books are sold!
To order, call 800-872-5627, or visit us at everything.com

Everything® is a registered trademark of Adams Media Corporation.